THE
COMPANION GUIDE
TO THE
SHABBAT
PRAYER SERVICE

Featuring Select~
and Explanations

MOSHE I. SORSCHER

Companion Guide to the

SHABBAT PRAYER SERVICE

ISBN # 1-880582-19-8

Library of Congress Cataloging-in-Publication Data
Sorscher, Moshe I.
Companion guide to the Shabbat prayer service / by Moshe I. Sorscher p. cm.
"Featuring synopses and explanations of significant prayers, selected transliterations,
parables & essays."   ISBN 1-880582-19-8
1. Siddur. Sabbath. 2. Sabbath--Liturgy. 3. Sabbath in rabbinical literature. 4. Jewish
parables. 5. Judaism--Liturgy. I. Siddur. Sabbath. Selections. II. Title.
BM675.S3Z797 1998   296.4'5--dc21
98-36893 CIP

THE JUDAICA PRESS, Inc.
123 Ditmas Avenue Brooklyn, NY 11218
718-972-6200   800-972-6201   info@judaicapress.com
www.judaicapress.com

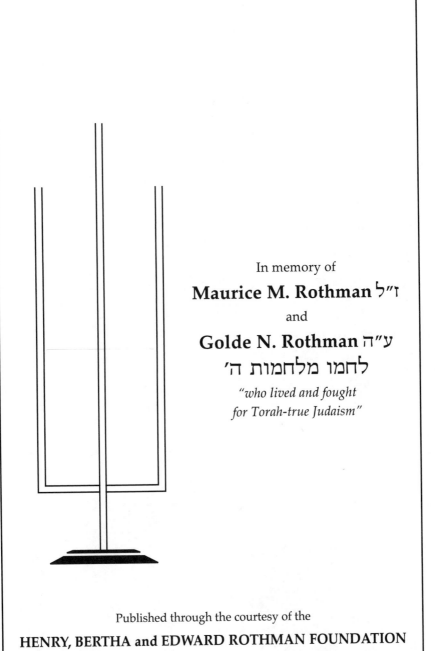

In memory of

Maurice M. Rothman ז"ל

and

Golde N. Rothman ע"ה

לחמו מלחמות ה׳

*"who lived and fought
for Torah-true Judaism"*

Published through the courtesy of the

HENRY, BERTHA and EDWARD ROTHMAN FOUNDATION

Rochester, NY • Circleville, OH • Cleveland, OH

Dedicated
in loving memory of

Mrs. Jennie Sorscher

שיינדעל בת ר' יהודה לייב, ע"ה

She engaged in gemilut chasadim,
chevra kadishah, limud Torah,
nichum aveilim, hachnasat orchim,
tefillah and tzedakah with every
fiber of her body and soul
all the days of her life

❧

May her memory be blessed

The Sorscher Family

ℐ *Table of Contents* ℱ

Foreword

"Open up for me the gates of righteousness so that I may enter and praise G-d. This is the gate to G-d, the righteous may enter therein" (Psalms 118:19).

It is not easy for a Jew to approach his Maker. He must first learn the art of prayer. Prayer, more than just words, requires thoughts as well. But more than appropriate thoughts, prayer requires words too. Only the right combination of heartfelt thoughts and reverent words can truly open the gates of Heaven and allow the outpouring of the soul to reach G-d. It is this art of prayer that has been lost to many today. Understanding and using the *Siddur*, the Jewish prayerbook, is the key. The *Siddur* can inspire and transform our thoughts into potent prayers that can pass through the gates of Heaven.

We hope that this Companion Guide will serve to open the *Siddur* to an audience for whom until now the *Siddur* was looked upon as a closed, mysterious and forbidding book. The inspiration for this Guide comes from the Beginner's Service at The Young

Israel of Flatbush, led by the author, Mr. Moshe Sorscher, who, with G-d's help, has been successful in teaching the art of prayer.

Kenneth Auman
Rabbi, Young Israel of Flatbush

Acknowledgements

This booklet is the third in a series of guides that I have compiled for the benefit of Jews who are uncomfortable and unfamiliar with the Prayer Service and who would like to learn more about the Prayers, their meaning and application.

Following the immensely successful *Companion Guides to the Rosh Hashanah and Yom Kippur Prayer Services*, it is my hope that this outline will assist the newcomer to the Synagogue and heighten his or her appreciation and understanding of the liturgy for the Sabbath morning.

The publication of these booklets came about as a result of the Outreach Program of my Synagogue, Young Israel of Flatbush in Brooklyn, New York, of which I am the co-ordinator. Our organization has dedicated itself to reaching out to our fellow Jews and to help and acquaint them with the magnificent heritage and traditions of the Jewish People.

The words are not easily available to express thanks and appreciation to the Young Israel for the opportunity I have been given to get involved in the noble work of Kiruv. Our program was fostered by the National Jewish Outreach Program and I am grateful to Rabbis Ephraim Buchwald and Yitzchak Rosenbaum for their inspiration in helping our program from its infancy. It has only been several years, yet we have been instrumental in changing the lives of scores of individuals.

I also wish to recognize the assistance and inspiration rendered by our spiritual leader, Rabbi Kenneth Auman, who has reviewed the manuscript and made many suggestions, all of which I have included. In addition, I wish to thank the administration and the very dedicated members of our committee for their wholehearted support and co-operation.

I further wish to express my deep appreciation to the Henry, Bertha and Edward Rothman Foundation, whose generosity made the publication of this Companion Guide possible. May they continue to have the merit to sponsor additional projects of this type. Thanks also to Zisi Berkowitz who typeset this book and to Bonnie Goldman and Aryeh Mezei of Judaica Press who worked hard to help shape the final result.

I am also grateful to my dear wife Naomi and my family for their continued patience and support in providing me with the atmosphere conducive to the writing of this booklet.

And, finally, my deepest and humblest thanks are reserved for the King of Kings, for the Creator of all things, Who has blessed me with the opportunity and selected me as the one to be involved in reaching out and touching hundreds of Jews. May I only be worthy to merit His continued blessings.

Moshe I. Sorscher

Preface

This edition of *The Companion Guide to the Shabbat Prayer Service* has been prepared to help you become more acquainted with the Shabbat Prayer Service. The Shabbat service is often daunting to the beginner—there's a lot to learn and it's all in Hebrew! I've included an outline in the hope that if you begin to understand the structure of the prayers, you will find that following the actual service will become much easier, even if you don't read Hebrew.

For the benefit of worshippers whose Hebrew reading is minimal, I have included an English transliteration of selected hymns and liturgical passages. For the transliteration, I used the Sephardic pronunciation since that is what is commonly used in spoken Modern Hebrew. Essays and inspirational stories are interspersed covering a wide range of prayer related topics.

If you are using this booklet along with a *Siddur*, we have provided handy page references for; the ArtScroll *Siddur* (**A**), the Birnbaum *Siddur* for Shabbat (**B**), the Birnbaum combined daily and Shabbat prayer book (**BC**), the Lubavitch *Siddur* (**L**) and the De Sola Pool *Siddur* (**DP**).

Feel free to use the guide in any way best suited for you. You may find it useful to have both the *Siddur* and the guide opened at the appropriate place and to glance back and forth from one to the other, or to refer to the guidebook only for the transliterations or the explanations of the prayers. Beginning Hebrew readers will find the transliterations very helpful as a phonetic guide.

All of the above was designed to help readers gain a better understanding of the Shabbat services so that the prayers could be appreciated more deeply.

Moshe I. Sorscher

The Significance of Shabbat

— ᚦ ᚦ —

Why is Shabbat so important? What is the significance of this day?

Judaism is a vast sea of ethical, moral and religious practices and observances. Judaism has bestowed countless ethical and moral teachings upon the world. But the ritual aspects, the observance of G-d's commandments, through the Biblical laws of Shabbat, *kashrut, mezuzah*, holidays, etc., were given only to the Jewish people.

Of all these rituals, observance of Shabbat is what most greatly distinguishes the Jewish People from the other nations of the world. The essence of this day is that in six days "G-d created the heaven and the earth, and on the seventh day He rested" (Exod. 20:11). He then made Shabbat a sign between Himself and the Jewish People, and commanded us to remember and observe the Shabbat day and make it holy.

The Torah mentions the observance of Shabbat more times than any other holiday, including Yom Kippur, thereby signifying the tremendous importance given to this commandment. In fact, the observance of Shabbat is so important, that it is listed in the Ten Commandments. In addition, the Talmud, the vast storehouse of Jewish law and lore, devotes hundreds of pages to the intricate laws of how Shabbat should be properly observed, and the procedures, opinions and practices of Shabbat are discussed and debated in great detail.

What is this idea of "rest" all about? What does it mean to rest? Why is this concept so important?

Once each week, Jews spend a day reinforcing their belief in the Creator. For as long as Shabbat is observed, G-d will continue to be a force in a Jew's life. However, while appreciating the importance and significance of Shabbat, many people remain confused about how best to observe it. They may wonder what the idea of resting is all about. They may think of rest as a day off from work, or as a time to enjoy a leisurely activity, or do things where no actual physical work is apparent, such as watching television.

The Torah states that G-d rested on the seventh day. This notion may seem ridiculous — was G-d tired from the six days of creation? Was creating the world such hard work for Him? This is unlikely; rather, G-d rested in the spiritual sense by creating the concept of rest, the idea of cessation of work. Therefore, the Shabbat was blessed and became a day of holiness and purity. It has become much more than simply a day of stopping our weekday pursuits; it has become a symbol of our belief in G-d and our desire to emulate Him. Just as G-d ceased from working on Shabbat and rested by not interfering with the work of creation, so do we, in our love of and belief in G-d, do likewise. Our Sages of the Talmud, derived thirty-nine major types of work forbidden on Shabbat [derived from the thirty-nine forms of labor involved in the constuction of the Tabernacle (Exod. ch. 25-28)]. From these, they further deduced many more additional acts of forbidden work. Some of these may seem very trivial, such as striking a match, or picking an apple from a tree; yet as small as some of them may seem in our eyes, what they stand for is a spiritual change from mundane pursuits, into the spiritual world of rest.

What is it like to observe Shabbat? What about the rituals? Isn't it difficult with all the restrictions?

Our Rabbis tell us that Shabbat is like a taste of the World-to-Come. Shabbat is a gift to the Jewish people and is the closest concept we have to the days of the Messiah when eternal peace will rule the world. No wonder we greet each other on Shabbat with "Shabbat Shalom," which means may you have a peaceful Shabbat. When one observes Shabbat, one is at peace, not only with other people, but with one's Creator as well. This, therefore, is the essence of the observance of our holiest day of the week—to spend it in peaceful and spiritual pursuits, free from our hectic daily routine.

On Friday afternoon all are busy with preparations for the coming Shabbat. Our homes have been cleaned, and we have bathed and set the table with our finest china and silver. The aroma of Shabbat cooking fills the air. When the candles are lit, all of a sudden one's home is transformed into a spiritual setting. There is suddenly a quiet peacefulness throughout the house.

Enjoy the warm glow of the candles; recite the Kiddush, the sanctification over a cup of wine; savor the delicious taste of the challah; enjoy the special Shabbat foods. While sitting at the beautifully-decked Shabbat table, discuss the Torah portion of the week or other holy pursuits. Don't discuss weekday problems. Sing Shabbat hymns and songs and spend quality time with your family and friends—time that seems impossible to find during the week. Don't be disturbed by the sound of the telephone, or the television, but enjoy the spiritual nature of our most holy of days, a day given only to G-d's chosen people.

On Shabbat morning, go to Synagogue and spend the morning in prayer and study. Hear the reading of the Torah and learn its relevant messages for today. Upon returning home, once again enjoy a leisurely Shabbat meal, feel the spirit of the day, sing additional hymns and recite the *Bircat Hamazon*, the Grace After Meals. You will surely feel rejuvenated by this magnificent day.

As the day wanes and the sun begins to set, we feel somewhat saddened, yet there is always the next Shabbat to look forward to. We then conduct the parting *Havdalah*, or Separation, ceremony. The fire and spices remind us that an extra soul stayed with us for a full day and is leaving us, but the glory and splendor of the Shabbat has reinvigorated us for the trying times that may lie ahead of us in the coming week.

Outline and Structure of the Shabbat Prayer Services

Good Shabbos!
Shabbat Shalom!

This outline has been prepared to help you become more acquainted with the Shabbat Prayer Service.

Erev Shabbat—Friday Afternoon

Minchah—The Friday Afternoon Prayer
Shemoneh Esray—The *Amida*, The Silent Devotion

Kabbalat Shabbat—Welcoming The Shabbat

Kabbalat Shabbat—Welcoming the Shabbat
  Introductory Psalms
  L'chah Dodi—Come my Beloved
  Concluding Psalms

Maariv—The Evening Service

Barchu—Blessing G-d
The *Shema*—Declaration of Faith
Shemoneh Esray—The *Amida*, The Silent Devotion
Concluding hymns

Shacharit—The Morning Service

Birchot Hashachar—Morning Blessings
Pesukay D'zimrah—Psalms of Praise
The *Shema* and its blessings—Declaration of Faith
Shemoneh Esray—The *Amida*, The Silent Devotion

Chazan's repetition of *Shemoneh Esray*
  Kedushah—Sanctification of G-d's Name

Kriyat HaTorah—The Torah Service

Removal of the Torah from the *Aron*
The Torah Reading
The *Haftarah*—Reading from the Prophets
Additional Prayers
Returning the Torah to the *Aron*

Mussaf—The Additional Service

Shemoneh Esray—The *Amida,* The Silent Devotion
Chazan's Repetition of the *Shemoneh Esray*
  Kedushah—Sanctification of G-d's Name

Mincha—The Afternoon Service

Introductory paragraphs
Torah Reading
Shemoneh Esray—The *Amida,* The Silent Devotion
Chazan's Repetition of the *Shemoneh Esray*
  Kedushah—Sanctification of G-d's Name

Maariv—The Evening Service

Barchu—Blessing G-d
The *Shema*—Declaration of Faith
Shemoneh Esray—The *Amida,* The Silent Devotion
Havdalah—Parting ceremony (recited at the close of
  the Sabbath)

The Purpose of Prayer

Prayer is essentially an outpouring of joy, thanks, awe, happiness, agony and gratitude. Prayer encourages us to express our emotions to G-d, not only voluntarily, but also, as an obligation. We are obligated to serve G-d, to love Him, to fear Him, to extol His virtues, and to worship Him, all of which are various forms of prayer.

In our prayers, we often address G-d as Our Father Our King, or as Our Father in Heaven, since we are regarded by G-d as His children and we regard Him as our Father. In addition to praying to G-d for the things we want and need, such as health, sustenance, happiness and *nachas*, we also pray for our mundane concerns.

Many questions come to mind about prayer. Why, for example, do we pray to G-d for our needs? Doesn't G-d know what we need better than we do? Doesn't G-d know what's best for us? Does G-d really need our prayers? And finally, does G-d really answer our prayers?

We can find the answers to these questions in different sources. G-d wants us to pray to Him because it is our way of acknowledging His glory and greatness. By asking G-d for everything we need, we express our belief in Him as the Supreme Being, as the only one who can answer our requests. This is the true meaning of prayer.

G-d wants us to pray to Him. He wants to hear our prayers said with complete sincerity and earnest devotion. The Torah relates that G-d revealed to Abraham that his seed would be as numerous as the stars in heaven. Yet, when Abraham's son Isaac and his wife Rebecca were childless, the Torah tells us that they both prayed to G-d for children. Weren't they aware that the future generations would flow through them? If they knew that they were to be the progenitors of the Jewish Nation, was it necessary to pray to G-d? The answer is, yes, of course, they knew, but in any case G-d desires to hear the prayers of the righteous who find favor in the eyes of the Lord. Hence, Rebecca was barren at first, but after listening to the supplications of His loved ones, G-d answered their prayers.

Similarly, we have been commanded to pray to G-d, not for *His* sake, but for *our* sake. G-d doesn't need our prayers; we need our prayers. We need them in order to make us better people. G-d desires our prayers, in order for us to become better people. We must acknowledge that through G-d alone we were given the opportunity to partake of His goodness and generosity. It is through G-d's mercy and kindness that we have received what we need. We should express our gratitude to Him many times a day, for we are dependent upon Him, not He upon us. Before we eat, we make a blessing; before we perform a commandment, we say a prayer; after we partake of His goodness, we thank Him.

We express our thanks through praise, or by reciting Psalms, by doing acts of kindness, like giving charity and performing other such good deeds. These are also character building aids.

Even in times of distress we are duty bound to pray to G-d and express our belief that everything He does is right. For even if we do not understand G-d's ways, we believe that G-d is good, His ways are good and whatever He does is for the good. If we suffer, then we must pray to G-d that He relieve us of our suffering. If we are sick, we must pray to G-d to heal us. And finally, when we know and feel that G-d has helped us (and make no mistake—help and salvation come only from G-d), then we must thank G-d in our prayers. Even if we think that assistance and help came from another source or through natural causes, we must strengthen our belief and conviction that although help may have come that way, it did so only because G-d so directed it.

Thus, prayer is called Service of the Heart (*Avodah Sheh-b'laiv*) for it is an expression of our deepest feelings. It comes directly from our heart—with complete and absolute sincerity.

Prayer and Its Origins

Ever since the days of the Patriarchs—Abraham, Isaac and Jacob—prayer has become a method whereby individuals can commune with their Maker. During the days of Moses, the Children of Israel cried out to G-d for salvation. There is much evidence that in the time of the Judges and Prophets, the people also prayed to G-d.

In the First Temple era, prayer was informal and very individual. Maimonides explains that an articluate individual would pray eloquently and frequently, while a simple person would pray less often and with greater simplicity.

After the destruction of the First Temple in 423 BCE, when the Jews were exiled and dispersed they could no longer pray as cohesively as before. During the seventy year period of exile, previous methods of prayer gradually were forgotten and prayer became a somewhat disorganized and informal experience.

Seventy years later, when the Second Temple was built, many Jews returned to Israel, and the great sage and scribe, Ezra, found a need to establish a set order of prayer. Together with the 120 men of the Great Assembly, he established the eighteen benedictions, known to us today as the *Shemoneh Esray* or *Amidah*. Various other additions were later inserted, such as the *Shema* and its blessings and various Psalms. At this time they also created set times for prayer in the morning, afternoon, and evening. Throughout this period, prayer became more formal and gradually Jews began to pray together in Synagogues.

At first the prayers were recited from memory. In the 9th century the first written *Siddur* was compiled by Rav Amram

Gaon, the head of the Yeshiva in Sura, Babylon. Later editions were written wherever Jews lived—following their local customs. The first printed *Siddur* actually appeared in Italy in 1486 and later versions were prepared in various parts of the world. Of course, today hundreds of different editions exist, many in accordance with customs of Sefardic, Ashkenazic or Chassidic Jewry.

Prayer on a Regular Basis

At the beginning of the era of the Second Temple the men of the Great Assembly instituted the thrice daily prayers. In order to relate worship to the concept of Service of the Heart, they instituted stations (*ma-amadot*) whereby all of Israel was involved in the Temple Service. The Priests (*Kohanim*) actually performed the Service; the Levites (*Leviyim*) stood on a platform and recited Psalms, and the Israelites (*Yisraelim*) appointed delegates who recited special prayers and scriptural passages. Prayer in Temple times, therefore, was associated with the daily offerings taking place in the Temple. Now that we no longer are privileged to have the Temple, our prayers must substitute for those offerings as well.

Our Sages determined that we must recite formal prayers three times daily. The morning Service (*Shacharit*), the afternoon Service (*Mincha*) and the evening Service (*Maariv* or *Arvit*). On the Sabbath, *Rosh Chodesh* and festivals, we also recite the Additional Service (*Mussaf*).

In the Talmud we find that each of our forefathers instituted one of the daily prayers: Abraham—*Shacharit*, Isaac—*Mincha* and Jacob—*Maariv*. Abraham's method of prayer included rising early in the morning to do G-d's bidding. He served G-d with love (*ahavah*) and distinguished himself with kindness (*chesed*).

Isaac, we learned, meditated in the fields before evening; this was his form of prayer. He worshiped G-d with awe (*yirah*) and excelled in the quality of justice (*din*).

At night, Jacob's prayer consisted of his "encounter" with G-d at the site where he dreamt of the ladder. He served G-d with mercy (*rachamim*), and distinguished himself with truth (*emet*). Jacob's ladder also represents our prayers and the various levels of communication with G-d, which can be measured in the steps of a ladder.

As G-d's children and the children of the Patriarchs, we invoke their names three times daily in the *Shemoneh Esray*. We have inherited their qualities of love and kindness, justice and fear, and truth and mercy, which enable us to pray to G-d with sincerity, devotion and reverence. In our prayers we invoke the qualities of our forefathers in the hope that G-d will favor us and act accordingly with us in His qualities of kindness, goodness and forgiveness.

Another purpose of prayer is to establish a relationship with G-d. For example, we should not pray only when we have a special reason to do so, i.e., when we recover from an illness or when we have lost a family member, or when we are particularly grateful. G-d should be worshiped regularly. This is similar to the fact that we cannot be parents to our children only on certain occasions; we must be parents all the time. Similarly we are the children of G-d at all times.

Prayer, on a daily basis, permeates our days and lives. Just as we need food to feed our bodies on a regular basis, so too we need prayer to feed our souls.

Prayer, therefore, becomes a way of life, a duty of the heart, a service to G-d. The ability to achieve a special closeness and spirituality with G-d is achieved through reaching an elevated state of mind, which can only be accomplished when prayer is recited on a continuous and daily schedule.

Prayer and the Synagogue

Although prayer in any form is acceptable, and even though our obligation is fulfilled if we pray alone, prayers made by at least ten men (a *minyan*) together are far more effective than those made by an individual. Whenever ten people pray together, the Divine Presence (the *Shechinah*) rests among them. Private prayer, no matter how fervently and devoutly offered, cannot compare to Congregational prayer. Many of our most important prayers, such as *Barchu, Kaddish, Kedushah*, and the Torah reading, cannot be recited unless a *minyan* is present. It is with the atmosphere of the

Holy Ark, the *Aron*, where the Torah and other items are located, that our prayers can be more readily acceptable to G-d. Even if one does not understand the Service, through worship with a *minyan*, one's prayers can be lifted to greater heights in a Congregational setting.

With communal prayer, we can approach G-d through the Congregation of Israel. We therefore pray in the plural and use a fixed set of prayers (also called *Nussach*) so that all of us are saying the same words to express our individual needs at the same time.

Prayer in the Hebrew Language

Any language is acceptable if one does not know Hebrew—as long as prayers are recited with sincerity and intense devotion (*kavanah*). This is true, however, only on an individual level.

Our Sages decreed that Congregational prayer must be in Hebrew, the language of our Torah, the Prophets and the Holy Writings. Even when the Jews were exiled, Hebrew was still retained as the Holy Language (*Lashon HaKodesh*), because it was used only for Torah study, worship, and writings. The Men of the Great Assembly insisted that when prayers are offered in a Congregation, they must be recited in Hebrew.

Wherever the Jews are dispersed, in countries all over the globe, even though their daily language may be Italian, French, Spanish or Russian, etc., in the Synagogue, prayers are still in Hebrew. Hebrew was, and still is, the common denominator that unites Jews. Were it not for our common language that has held us together through slavery, dispersion, pogroms, exile and hardship, one of the most powerful links with our glorious past might have been lost.

Prayer and the Cantor

The Cantor (*Chazan*), whether professionally trained or not, leads the Congregation and acts as the Congregation's interceder with G-d. The Cantor pleads with the Almighty that his prayers, as well as those of the Congregation, be accepted and answered. His task is one of great responsibility and requires knowledge and understanding of the prayers as well as the ability to motivate the Congregation to achieve greater heights.

The Cantor is also known as the representative of the Congregation (*Shaliach Tzibur*). Years ago, when the people did not know how to read and didn't understand the prayers, the Cantor would recite them and the Congregation would listen intently. A translator was present as well. In some Synagogues the Cantor may be a lay leader, untrained in music. In other Synagogues he may have a powerful and melodic voice. In either case, the Cantor must have an ability to motivate and inspire. More importantly the role he plays must intensify his beliefs and help in uplifting his prayers, and he must be acceptable to the Congregation.

A Prayer

Let us hope and pray that our prayers gain for us greater insight and understanding and reach the highest spheres of the Heavens. May we all merit through our prayers all the blessings in the storehouses of the Almighty—good health, sustenance, joy and happiness. May our prayers be answered and may our dreams become reality.

We pray that peace and goodwill will finally come for our beloved land of Israel and that the Temple in Jerusalem will be rebuilt speedily and in our day. Lastly, we pray that we will shortly see the coming of the Messiah and the redemption of our people from the four corners of the earth, Amen.

1 B

Customs of the Synagogue

The *Aron Kodesh* and the *Bimah*

In the Great Temple in Jerusalem the *Aron Kodesh*, or Ark, contained the original Ten Commandments. Today the Synagogue is suggestive of the Temple and the *Aron Kodesh*, which contains the Torah Scrolls, faces East towards Jerusalem, the site where our Holy Temple stood. The *Bimah*, or stage, is representative of the Altar where sacrifices were brought. The Cantor, also known as the *Chazan* or leader of the service, is suggestive of the High Priest also known as the *Kohen Gadol*. It was the *Kohen Gadol* who conducted the sacrificial procedures in the days of the Temple.

The *Mechitza*: Separation

The *mechitza* serves as a separation between males and females so that we may pray without distractions, thus making our prayers more meaningful and acceptable to G-d. The *mechitza* originated in the days of the Temple when separate sections were constructed for the women. Today our Synagogue represents the Temple. In fact, the Talmud indicates exactly when men and women should be separated in order to avoid distractions; one of these times is during prayer. In addition the separation helps us concentrate on our prayers, and offers us the ability to communicate with G-d with greater reverence.

The *Yarmulka* or *Kipah*: Head Covering

The headcovering or skull cap (also known as *yarmulka* or *kipah*) for the male is simply a sign of respect worn by observant Jews to indicate that the spirit of G-d is constantly upon them. Any male, Jew or Gentile, entering the Synagogue Sanctuary during a Service should wear a head covering. In some Synagogues many men also wear hats during the Service. The skull cap has no mystical meaning and serves only as a covering however, it has become a universal symbol. A head covering has psychological significance, as it announces the wearer's acknowlegement that there is a Holy Presence above him. Married women cover their hair as a sign of modesty.

The *Tallit*: Prayer Shawl

This fringed garment is derived from the verses in the *Shema* prayer, "Bid them make fringes in the four corners of their garments." The purpose of the *tallit*, or prayer shawl, is to remind us of the commandments which are symbolized by the knots in the fringes. Only Jewish adult males wear the *tallit*. In some Synagogues, a Jew dons a *tallit* for the first time when he is married. It is also the practice of males to wear a small *tallit* as an undergarment so that he will always be reminded to observe the *mitzvot*.

How To Use This Guide

The **Shabbat Companion Guide** is to be used together with a Shabbat *Siddur* (prayer book). In order to make this guide accessible to as many people as possible, we have indicated the corresponding pages in the *ArtScroll Siddur (Ashkenaz), Birnbaum Siddur (Ashkenaz*—both the combined daily and Shabbat edition and the Shabbat edition), the *Lubavitch Siddur* (i.e., *nusach Ha-Ari*) and the *De Sola Pool Siddur*.

The page numbers are preceded by the letters:

A for the *ArtScroll Siddur*

B for the *Birnbaum* (Shabbat edition) *Siddur*

BC for the *Birnbaum* combined (i.e., the combined daily and Shabbat edition) *Siddur*

L for the *Lubavitch Siddur*

DP for the *De Sola Pool Siddur*

2

Erev Shabbat—
Mincha
Friday Afternoon

ℳ MINCHA ℛ
("Afternoon Service")

A 232 B 1 BC 157 L 96 DP 3

he Friday Afternoon Service preceding the Shabbat is
exactly the same as any weekday Afternoon Service. The
service consists of an introductory Psalm, *Ashray* (Fortunate),
followed by the *Shemoneh Esray* (*Amidah* or Silent Devotion)
and concludes with *Alaynu*.

When *Mincha* is recited in the Synagogue, there are a few
additions to the Afternoon Service. Prior to the recital of the *Shemoneh Esray*, the *Chazan* chants the Half *Kaddish*. In addition,
the *Chazan* will repeat the *Shemoneh Esray*, and the *Kedushah*
(Sanctification) is inserted into the repetition. In fact, the *Kedushah* is the most important part of the prayer service since it is a
unified moment when the Congregation rises and recites praise to
G-d. The Congregation follows the *Chazan*'s repetition, answering
Amen where applicable.

ॐ HADLAKAT NAYROT ॐ
("Lighting Shabbat Candles")

A 296 **B** 23 **BC** 221 **L** 127 **DP** 599

As the sun begins to set on Friday evening, we usher in Shabbat by lighting candles. Although the commandment to light candles is not Scriptural, this beautiful custom is observed as if it were Biblically decreed. It has become one of the main symbols of Shabbat.

The purpose of the Shabbat candles is to bring light and enjoyment into the home. Since we cannot discern the last moment of a day, the Sages determined that Shabbat should be accepted early. In Jerusalem, the custom is to light candles 30-40 minutes before sundown. However, most Jewish communities light eighteen minutes before sunset.

Various customs exist concerning the number of candles lit. Everybody lights at least two candles, one of which corresponds to the positive commandments of Shabbat, and the other to the prohibitions. Some people light seven candles which represents the seven days of the week, or ten candles representing the Ten Commandments. Still others light one candle for each family member, thereby showing that each person brings a special light to the world.

ॐ HOW TO LIGHT SHABBAT CANDLES ॐ

1. Light candles near the table where you will be eating your Shabbat meal so that you can enjoy their glow while you eat.

2. Be sure to light candles in a safe manner. Candles should always be out of the reach of young children, away from curtains and not exposed to an open window. A large metal tray beneath the candles can be added as an extra precaution.

3. Shabbat candles can be purchased in various quantities. A large box with seventy-two candles is most common. Also available are candles sold in glass containers. These candles have a nice, even flame and turn to liquid as they burn.

4. It is customary to hold your hands in front of your face and move them in a circular manner toward your face after lighting the

candles and before saying the blessing. This symbolizes your readiness to accept Shabbat into your life.

5. Cover your eyes while saying the following blessing:

"Baruch atah Adonai, Elohaynu melech ha-lolam, asher kidshanu b'mitzvotav v'tzeevanu l'hadlik nayr shel Shabbat."

Only after reciting the blessing and accepting Shabbat, should we enjoy the light of the candles.

☙ *A Precious Gift* ❧

When G-d was ready to give the Torah, He called the Israelites and said to them, "My children, I have a precious gift to give you if you keep the Torah and its commandments."

The Israelites asked, "What is this gift?"

G-d said, "The World to Come."

The Israelites then asked G-d, "Is there anything in this world like the World to Come?"

G-d said, "The Shabbat is a taste of the World to Come!"

☙ *The Holy Shabbat* ❧

There are three things called Holy (*Kadosh*).

One is the Shabbat, as it is written, "You shall keep the Shabbat, for it is holy to you" (Exod. 31:14).

The second is Israel, as it is written, "Israel is holy to G-d" (Jer. 2:3).

The third is G-d, as it is said, "You are Holy, dwelling among the praises of Israel" (Ps. 22:4).

All these three are said to be equal. If the Israelites who are called *holy* keep the Shabbat which is *holy*, then G-d, Who is *holy*, will make His Divine Presence dwell among them.

3

Kabbalat Shabbat & Maariv
The Evening Service

✎ KABBALAT SHABBAT ✎
("Welcoming the Shabbat")

A 308 B 23 BC 237 L 128 DP 31

The Talmud (Shab. 119a) describes the beautiful and touching way in which the great Sages, Rabbi Chanina and Rabbi Yannai, would welcome the Shabbat. The Rabbis would put on their best Shabbat clothes and exclaim, "Come and let us go forth to welcome the Shabbat Queen."

In the 16th century, the Kabbalists who lived in Safed, in northern Israel, inspired by these Talmudic Sages, instituted the *Kabbalat Shabbat* Service to welcome the Shabbat, and this was later incorporated into the Friday Evening Service.

Kabbalat Shabbat consists of three sections. The first is the recital of six psalms, each of which symbolizes a day of the week, and each day alludes to a different day of creation. These are followed by the beautiful poem of *L'chah Dodi* ("Come my Beloved"). The Safed Kabbalists would dress in white and walk together to the gates of the city, singing *L'chah Dodi* to welcome the Shabbat, and then return to town escorting the Shabbat bride. The final part of the "Welcoming of the Shabbat" consists of two psalms, recited together, which represent the seventh day, the Shabbat, when G-d rested from creating.

ঞ Introductory Psalms ৰ

Psalm 95—*L'chu N'ran'nah* ("Come let us sing")—This Psalm is a call to Israel to worship the Creator of the world. The psalm concludes with a plea that if Israel will heed G-d's voice and follow G-d's way, the Promised Land will be reached.

Psalm 96—*Shiru La'adonai Shir Chadash* ("Sing to Hashem, a new song")—This Psalm is Israel's rousing call to the nations of the world to worship G-d. The word *shiru* (sing) is mentioned three times which corresponds to the three times each day—in the morning prayers, afternoon prayers, and evening prayers—that Jews sing praise to G-d.

Psalm 97—*Adonai Malach Tagayl Ha-aretz* ("Hashem will reign and the Earth will rejoice")—This Psalm contains a description of the future, of the Messianic Era, when great happiness and rejoicing will abound.

Psalm 98—*Mizmor, Shiru La'Adonai* ("A Psalm, sing to Hashem")—This is a call to proclaim the Lord as the Supreme King for all the wonders He has done. "With trumpets and the sound of a shofar, raise your voices before the King, the Lord. The sea and its fullness will roar. Rivers will clap hands together, mountains will sing joyously."

Psalm 99—*Adonai Malach Yirg'zu Amim* ("When G-d will reign, nations will tremble")—This Psalm describes how nations will tremble as they will realize the Divine judgment that awaits them. The Psalmist invokes the name of Moses, Aaron and Samuel, who were among those who called upon G-d and who were answered by Him.

Psalm 29—*Mizmor L'David* ("A Psalm to David")—This Psalm alludes to both the Shabbat and the Torah, since the Torah was given at Mount Sinai on Shabbat. For this reason, we chant *Mizmor L'David* when the Torah is returned to the *Aron* after the Torah reading on Shabbat Morning.

The Congregation rises for the recital of this psalm.
It is either sung or recited aloud with deep concentration.

MIZMOR L'DAVID
("A Psalm to David")

A 314 **B** 27 **BC** 241 **L** 131 **DP** 37

This Psalm contains G-d's name eighteen times, and mentions *Kol Adonai* (G-d's voice) seven times. The number eighteen corresponds to the eighteen blessings that are part of the *Amidah*. The number seven corresponds to the seven days of Creation.

Mizmor L'David
Havu La'Adonai b'nay aylim,
havu La'Adonai kavod va-oz,
havu La'Adonai kavod sh'mo,
hishta-cha-vu la'Adonai b'hadrat kodesh.

Kol Adonai al hamahyim,
El haka-vod hir-im Adonai al mahyim rabim.

Kol Adonai ba-ko-ach,
kol Adonai b'hadar,
kol Adonai shovayr arazim,
vai-sha-bayr Adonai et arzay halvanon.

Va-yarkidaym k'mo aygel,
l'vanon v'siryon k'mo ven r'aymim.

Kol Adonai chotzayv lahavot aysh,
kol Adonai yachil midbar,
yachil Adonai midbar kadaysh,
kol Adonai y'cholayl ayalot.

Va-ye-chesof y'arot,
uv'haychalo kulo omayr kavod.

Adonai lamabul yashav,
vayayshev Adonai melech l'olam.
Adonai oz l'amo yeetayn,
Adonai y'varaych et amo vashalom.

℣ L'CHAH DODI ℣
("Come my Beloved")

A 316 **B** 29 **BC** 243 **L** 131 **DP** 39

Kabbalat Shabbat continues with *L'chah Dodi*, a beautiful song alluding to the Shabbat bride. This poem was written by the 16th century kabbalist, Rabbi Shlomo Halevy. The initials of his name, Rabbi SH'LoMoH HaLeVY form the first letter of the eight stanzas. The song is devoted to our yearning for Jerusalem and the splendor of the Shabbat, which is compared to a bride or to a queen. The refrain, *"L'chah Dodi Likrat Kallah, P'nay Shabbat N'kablah"* (Come my beloved to greet the bride, let us welcome the presence of the Shabbat), is chanted after each stanza. The allusion to Shabbat as a bride is based on a *midrash* that the Jewish people are considered the groom and the Shabbat the bride. In most Synagogues, the entire poem is sung together by the *Chazan* and the Congregation. In other Synagogues, after the first refrain, each stanza is recited by the Congregation and repeated by the *Chazan*. Customs differ whether *L'chah Dodi* is sung while seated or standing. One should follow the custom of his or her Synagogue. In all Synagogues, the Congregation and the *Chazan* turn toward the door to greet the Shabbat bride as they sing the last stanza of this song.

L'chah dodi likrat kallah, p'nay Shabbat n'kablah.

**Shamor v'zachor b'deebur echad,
hishmee-anu El ham'yuchad,
Adonai echad ush'mo echad,
l'shaym ul'tiferet v'lit-heelah.**

L'chah dodi likrat kallah, p'nay Shabbat n'kablah.

**Likrat Shabbat l'chu v'naylchah,
kee hee m'kor habrachah,
mayrosh mikedem n'soochah,
sof maaseh b'machashava t'cheelah.**

L'chah dodi likrat kallah, p'nay Shabbat n'kablah.

**Mikdash melech ir m'luchah,
kumee tz'ee mitoch ha-hafaychah.**

rav lach shevet b'aymek habachah,
v'hu yachamol alayich chemlah.
L'chah dodi likrat kallah, p'nay Shabbat n'kablah.

Hitna-aree may-ahfar koomee,
livshee bigday tifartaych ahmee,
al yad ben yeeshai bayt halachmee,
karvah el nafshee g'alah.
L'chah dodi likrat kallah, p'nay Shabbat n'kablah.

Hitor'ree hitor'ree,
ki va oraych koomi oree,
ooree ooree shir dabayree,
k'vod Adonai alayich niglah.
L'chah dodi likrat kallah, p'nay Shabbat n'kablah.

Lo tayvoshee v'lo tikalmee,
mah tishto-cha-chee oomah teh-heh-mee,
bach yechesu aneeyay ahmee,
v'nivn'tah ir al teelah.
L'chah dodi likrat kallah, p'nay Shabbat n'kablah.

V'hayoo limshee-sah sho-sa-yich,
v'rachakoo kal m'val-ayich,
yasees alayich Elohayich
kimsos chatan al kallah.
L'chah dodi likrat kallah, p'nay Shabbat n'kablah.

Yamin oos'mol tifrotzee,
v'et Adonai ta-areetzee,
al yad ish ben partzee,
v'nism'cha v'nageelah.
L'chah dodi likrat kallah, p'nay Shabbat n'kablah.

(The entire Congregation and Chazan *turn to face the rear of the synagogue, and welcome the Shabbat bride. When chanting the words* Bo-ee Challah, *the Congregation bows slightly and turns back to its original place.)*

Bo-ee v'shalom ateret baalah,
gam b'simcha oov'tzahalah,

**toch emunay am s'gulah,
bo'ee challah, bo-ee challah.**

L'chah dodi likrat kallah, p'nay Shabbat n'kablah.

ৠ CONCLUSION OF KABBALAT SHABBAT ৰ

A 320 B 33 BC 247 L 133 DP 43

The final part of the welcoming of the Shabbat consists of two Psalms, *Mizmor Shir L'yom HaShabbat* ("A Song for the Shabbat Day"), Psalm 92, and *Adonai Malach Gayut Lavaysh* ("*Hashem* will have reigned"), Psalm 93. Psalm 92 was the song the Levites chanted in the Great Temple on Shabbat. Many say this Psalm was written by Adam, G-d's first human being. The theme of both Psalms is that G-d's greatness will be recognized in the future and that the Shabbat Day will be a day of rest for all eternity. These two Psalms discuss the seventh day when G-d rested from the Creation. As soon as these Psalms are said, the Congregation accepts the Shabbat upon themselves and ceases from all manner of forbidden work. If there are mourners in the Synagogue, the Mourner's *Kaddish* is recited following these Psalms *(see page 23)*.

The Congregation rises in preparation for the Borchu *and the* Maariv *Service.*

ৠ MAARIV ৰ
("Evening Service")

Abraham, Isaac and Jacob each had a major prayer attributed to him. *Shacharit* ("Morning Service") was attributed to Abraham, *Mincha* ("Afternoon Service") to Isaac, and *Maariv* ("Evening Service") to Jacob, who dreamt of a ladder, symbolizing prayer. The Hebrew name for *Maariv* is *Arvit*, meaning evening.

The *Chazan* begins the Evening Service with *Barchu*.

ৠ BARCHU ৰ
("Invitation to Congregation to bless G-d")

A 330 B 43 BC 257 L 135 DP 55

Barchu is the *Chazan*'s summons to the Congregation to bless G-d prior to reciting the *Shema*. This call acknowledges our realization that G-d is the source of all blessings. Like certain other parts of the prayer service (e.g., *Kaddish*, *Kedushah*, the Torah Reading), the recital of *Barchu* requires a *minyan*.

The Chazan *and Congregation bow slightly at the command* Barchu, *and everyone stands erect when G-d's name is recited.*

Chazan **Barchu Et Adonai Ham-vorach**
("Bless G-d, the Blessed One")

The Congregation again bows at the word Baruch *and straightens up at G-d's name.*

Cong. **Baruch Adonai Ham-vorach L'olam Va-ed**
("Blessed is G-d, the Blessed One for all of eternity")

This sentence is repeated by the Chazan.

℘ THE BLESSINGS PRECEDING THE SHEMA ℘

A 330 B 43 BC 257 L 135 DP 55

Following *Barchu*, two blessings precede the *Shema*. The first blessing, *Asher Bidvaro* ("Who, by His word"), describes G-d's control over nature and praises G-d as the Creator of the heavenly bodies and for His power to create night and day. This blessing concludes with the words *Hama-ariv Aravim* ("Who brings on evenings").

The second blessing, *Ahavat Olam* ("Eternal love"), said just prior to reciting the *Shema*, describes G-d's love for His people and praises G-d for giving us the Torah to study and obey, for it is the essence of our lives. This blessing concludes with the words *Ohayv Amo Yisrael* ("Who loves His nation Israel").

℘ THE SHEMA ℘
(Acceptance of G-d's Sovereignty)

A 330 B 43 BC 257 L 136 DP 57

The passage from Deuteronomy (6:4), "Hear O Israel, The Lord is our G-d, The Lord is One," and the three paragraphs that follow are part of both the daily morning and evening prayers. The *Shema* is the single most important sentence in the liturgy. It is not, in fact, a prayer, but rather an affirmation of the oneness of G-d.

So important is the *Shema* that it must be recited with undivid-

ॐ *Understanding Shema* ॐ

he *Shema* is the Jew's confession of faith and procla-
mation of the oneness and uniqueness of G-d. It is often
the first religious sentence a Jewish child is taught.

In Deuteronomy (6:6-7) we are told to recite the Shema twice
daily: "These words that I command you today shall be upon
your heart, and you shall impress them sharply upon your
children and speak of them when you sit in your house and when
you walk upon the way, when you lie down and when you get
up."

We are told in the *Talmud* (Berakhot 4b) that the *Shema*
should be recited in bed every night before going to sleep. The
Shema is also said by relatives and friends on behalf of a dying
Jew. And it is the last sentence to be uttered by Jews on their
deathbed.

Unknown numbers of Jewish martyrs met their deaths with
the words of the *Shema* on their lips. In the 2nd century C.E.,
while being tortured to death by the Romans, Rabbi Akiva
recited the first portion of the *Shema*. Rabbi Akiva said that he
welcomed his sufferings as a way to fulfill the commandment to
"love the Lord Thy G-d with all thy heart and with all thy soul,"
even if he had to pay with his life. As his flesh was being torn
from his body with iron combs, Rabbi Akiva recited the *Shema*
with a smile. His disciples said, "Our teacher, even to this point
you are happy to recite the *Shema*?" Rabbi Akiva replied, "All
my life I have been troubled by the verse 'with all thy soul.' I
said to myself, 'When will I have the opportunity of fulfilling
it?' Now that I have the opportunity shall I not fulfill it?" And so
Rabbi Akiva prolonged the word *echad* until he slipped out of
consciousness, and died while saying it.

The *Shema* so aptly summarizes the basic principles of Judaism that its first two paragraphs are inscribed on the parchment
scrolls of both the *mezuzah* and *tefillin*.

ed attention. To concentrate, it is traditional to cover or close one's eyes while reciting the verse. The recitation of the *Shema* represents the acceptance of G-d's absolute sovereignty.

SHEMA YISRAEL
("Hear O Israel")

Chazan and Cong. recite aloud, carefully enunciating each word.
Shema Yisrael, Adonai Elohaynu, Adonai Echad
("Hear O Israel, The Lord is our G-d, The Lord is One")

Chazan and Cong. recite in an undertone.
Baruch Shem K'vod Malchuto L'olam Va-ed
("Blessed be the name of the glory of His Kingdom forever and ever")

V'AHAVTA
("And you shall love")

A 332 B 43 BC 257 L 136 DP 57

This first paragraph of the *Shema* describes how we should love G-d with all our heart, with all our soul and with all our might, and in it we are commanded to convey this love to the next generation. This section also contains the two *mitzvot* ("commandments") of *tefillin* and *mezuzah*.

Cong. recites softly to themselves.
V'ahavta ayt Adonai Elohecha, b'chol l'vav'cha, uv'chol nafsh'cha, uv'chol m'odecha. V'hayu had'varim ha-ayleh, asher anochee m'tzav'cha hayom, al l'vavecha. V'sheenantam l'vanecha, v'deebarta bam, b'shivt'cha b'vaytecha, uv'lecht'cha vaderech, uv'shochb'cha uv'kumecha. Uk'shartam l'ot al yadecha, v'hayu l'totafot bayn aynecha. Uch'tavtam al m'zuzot baytecha, uvish'arecha.

V'HAYA
("And it will come to pass")

In the second paragraph we are commanded as a Jewish nation to accept G-d's commandments, and promised reward if we fulfill them, punishment if we do not. Again we are enjoined to teach these commandments to our children and to observe the *mitzvot* of *tefillin* and *mezuzah*.

Cong. recites softly to themselves.

V'haya im sha-moah tishm'u el mitzvotai, asher anochee m'tzaveh et-chem hayom, l'ahavah et Adonai Elohaychem ul'avdo, b'chol l'vavchem uv'chol nafsh'chem. V'natati m'tar artz'chem b'eeto, yoreh umalkosh, v'asafta d'ganecha, v'teerosh'cha v'yitz-harecha. V'natati aysev b'sadcha livhemtecha, v'achalta v'savata. Heeshamru lachem, pen yifteh l'vavchem, v'sartem va-avad'tem elohim achayrim, v'hishtachaveetem lahem. V'chara af Adonai bachem, v'atzar et hashamayim, v'lo yihyeh matar, v'ha-adamah lo teetayn et y'vulah, va-avadtem m'hayrah, may-al ha-aretz hatovah, asher Adonai notayn lachem. V'samtem et d'varai ayleh, al l'vavchem v'al nafsh'chem, uk'shartem otam l'ot al yedchem, v'hayu l'totafot bayn aynaychem. V'leemad'tem otam et b'naychem, l'dabayr bam, b'shivt'cha b'vaytecha, uv'lecht'cha vaderech, uv'shochb'cha uv'kumecha. Uch'tavtam al m'zuzot baytecha, uvish'arecha. L'ma-an yirbu y'maychem, veeymay v'naychem al ha-adamah asher nishba Adonai la-avotaychem latayt lahem, keeymay hashamayim al ha-aretz.

VAYOMER
("And G-d said")

The third paragraph details the laws of *tzitzit* ("fringes"), which serve to remind us of the Torah's precepts and recalls our exodus from Egypt.

Cong. recites softly to themselves.

Vayomer Adonai el Moshe laymor. Dabayr el B'nay Yisrael, v'amarta alayhem, v'asu lahem tzitzit, al kanfay vigdayhem l'dorotam, v'natnu al tzitzit hakanaf p'til t'chaylet. V'haya lachem l'tzitzit, ur'eetem oto, uz'chartem et kol mitzvot Adonai, va-aseetem otam. V'lo taturu acharay l'vavchem, v'acharay aynaychem asher atem zonim acharayhem.

L'ma-an tizk'ru, va-aseetem et kol mitzvotai, v'heyeetem
k'doshim laylohaychem. Ani Adonai Elohaychem,
asher hotzaytee etchem may-eretz Mitzrayim, lihyot
lachem laylohim, Ani

Make sure these final three words are said without interruption:

Adonai Elohaychem, emet.

☙ CONCLUDING BLESSINGS FOLLOWING THE SHEMA ☙

A 334 B 47 BC 261 L 137 DP 59

Two blessings follow the *Shema*. The first blessing refers to the
exodus of the Children of Israel from Egypt and the second
blessing describes the protection that G-d gives us under His
Succah of Peace. In the middle of the recitation of the first
blessing, Congregations usually sing the following praises of G-d:

MEE CHAMOCHAH

("Who is like You")

Cong. recites, Chazan *repeats, or sung in unison.*

Mee chamochah ba-aylim Adonai,
mee kamochah ne-edar bakodesh,
norah t'heelot o-say feleh.

ADONAI YIMLOCH

("G-d will reign")

Cong. recites, Chazan *repeats, or sung in unison.*

Adonai Yimloch L'olam Va-ed.

V'SHAMRU

("And they shall preserve")

A 336 B 49 BC 263 L 138 DP 61

The Congregation now rises and affirms the verses below
which are repeated by the *Chazan*. Following is a translation of
the verses: —"And the children of Israel shall observe the
Shabbat, to maintain the Shabbat as an everlasting covenant for
their generations. It is a sign forever between Me and the Children
of Israel, that in six days G-d made heaven and earth, and on the

seventh day He rested and was refreshed" (Exod. 31:16-17).

Cong. recites, Chazan *repeats.*

**V'shamru v'nay Yisrael et hashabbat,
la-asot et hashabbat l'dorotam b'rit olam.
Baynee uvayn B'nay Yisrael ot hee l'olam,
kee shayshet yamim asah Adonai
et hashamayim v'et ha-aretz,
uvayom hash'vee-ee shavat va-yee-nafash.**

☙ HALF KADDISH ☙

A 336 B 49 BC 263 L 138 DP 63

The Half *Kaddish*, written in Aramaic, was composed while the Jews were exiled in Babylonia. Its central idea is the revelation of G-d's kingship. In it we petition for G-d's kingdom to be established speedily. One of four different types of *Kaddish*, it connects various parts of the prayer service together. Here, it introduces the *Shemoneh Esray* (*Amidah*). The most important part of the *Kaddish* is the congregational response affirming G-d's name: *Amen. Y'hay sh'may rabbah m'varach...* ("May His great name be blessed forever and ever"), which should be recited aloud and fervently.

Chazan *recites:*
Yitgadal, v'yitkadash, sh'may rabbah. *Cong. responds* Amen.

**B'almah di-v'ra chirutay, v'yamlich malchutay,
b'chayaychon uv'yomaychon, u'v'chayay d'chol
bayt Yisrael, ba-agalah uvizman kareev,
v'imru, Amen.** *Cong. responds* Amen.

Chazan *and Cong. recite together:* **Y'hay sh'may rabbah m'varach,
l'alam ul'almay almahyah.**

Chazan *recites:*
**Yitbarach, v'yishtabach, v'yit-pa-ar, v'yit-romam,
v'yit-naseh, v'yit-hadar, v'yit-aleh, v'yit-halal,
sh'may d'kudshah, B'rich Hu.** *Cong. responds* B'rich Hu.

**L'aylah, min kol birchatah v'shiratah, tushb'chatah,
v'ne-chematah, da-amiran b'almah,
v'imru, Amen.** *Cong. responds* Amen.

ℳ SHEMONEH ESRAY–AMIDAH ℵ
(Silent Devotion)

A 338 B 51 BC 265 L 139 DP 63

The *Shemoneh Esray* or *Amidah* is the central part of the Evening Service. *Amidah,* another name for this prayer, means "standing," after the position one must take while saying it. *Shemoneh Esray* means "eighteen," which is the number of blessings originally included in the Silent Devotion of the weekday service. The name *Shemoneh Esray* has been retained as the name for all the silent devotional prayers, even though on the Shabbat and holidays the Silent Devotion contains only seven blessings.

The *Shemoneh Esray* is the only prayer recited at every single daily and holiday synagogue service throughout the year. Its seven Shabbat and Holiday benedictions and nineteen weekday blessings embrace the three dimensions necessary for Jewish prayer: Praise, Petition and Thanksgiving. The blessings of praise and thanksgiving are the same every day of the year. On the Shabbat and holidays, the weekday benedictions of petition are reduced from thirteen to one, since on these special days, our personal needs are provided for and there is no need to petition G-d for anything.

The following is a summary of the three sections of the *Shemoneh Esray*:

Praise—The first of the *Shemoneh Esray*'s three blessings recognizes G-d's glory. We approach G-d as the children of Abraham, Isaac and Jacob, with whom G-d made an eternal covenant. We come to G-d, Who is kind, supports the fallen, heals the sick and eventually restores life to the dead. G-d is holy and we, His children, recognize His omniscience.

Petition—This middle blessing expresses the holiness of the Shabbat day. This section contains several paragraphs relating to the Shabbat including the Biblical narrative of the seventh day and a request that G-d sanctify the Shabbat for us as an eternal heritage.

Thanksgiving—Having concluded our requests to G-d, we can now close the *Shemoneh Esray* with three blessings expressing

≈ *Reciting the Silent Devotion* ≈

his prayer is called either the *Amidah* ("standing") or the *Shemoneh Esray* ("eighteen"). There is evidence in the *Torah* that the blessings in the *Shemoneh Esray* date back to Abraham, Issac and Jacob, although the final form was arranged in Babylonia by the Rabbis of the Great Assembly.

At all times keep in mind that the intention of prayer is communication with G-d. Rabbi Eliezer ben Hyrcanus, a prominent 1st-century scholar, reminded his students: "When you pray, know before Whom you are standing."

The Rabbis prescribed a strict etiquette for how to stand before G-d when we pray, as follows:

1. Before praying we prepare to approach G-d—take three steps backwards (starting with your left foot) and then three steps forward. Then remain absolutely still with both feet together throughout the prayer (as a sign of respect and also to signify your earnest desire to speak to G-d).

2. Recite the prayer softly, articulating each word so that you hear yourself.

3. In the opening prayer, bend knees at the word *Baruch* ("Blessed"), then bow at the word *Attah* ("You"), straightening back up at the name of G-d. Do the same at the conclusion of the first blessing. The same procedure is repeated at the end of the *Shemoneh Esray*, at *Modim* ("We thank You"), bowing at the beginning and end of the blessing.

4. When you recite the words "He who makes peace," found in the next-to-last paragraph of the *Shemoneh Esray*, take three steps backwards, beginning with your left foot. Then bow three times, once to the left, once to the right, then forward. This symbolizes your departure from G-d's throne. Finally, take three steps forward and remain in place for a few seconds after the *Shemoneh Esray*.

our gratitude. This is similar to a petitioner withdrawing from a king's royal presence. This section includes a prayer for peace and a prayer asking for G-d's protection.

Many of us recite the *Amidah* softly, with lips moving, sometimes swaying as we pray, as an aid to our concentration, as it is most appropriate to pray the *Shemoneh Esray* with intense spiritual devotion. *Consult your* Siddur *for specific instructions and procedures as well as notes about which paragraphs are omitted or added.*

❧ FOLLOWING THE SHEMONEH ESRAY ❧

A 346 B 59 BC 273 L 142 DP 81

After the Silent Devotion, we recite a series of three short prayers with the theme of holiness and sanctity of the Shabbat.

VAY'CHULU
("Thus were finished")

Here are the verses found in Genesis 2:1-3, which recount G-d's completion of His six days of Creation and His blessing and sanctification of the Shabbat. In some synagogues, *Vayachulu* is recited by the Congregation and repeated by the *Chazan*. In others, however, the *Chazan* and Congregation sing these verses together.

"Now the heavens and the earth were completed and all their host. And G-d completed on the seventh day His work that He did, and He abstained on the seventh day from all His work that He did. And G-d blessed the seventh day and He hallowed it, because on it He abstained from all His work that G-d created to do."

**Vay'chulu hashamayim
v'ha-aretz v'chal tz'va-am.
Vay'chal Elohim bayom hash'vee-ee m'lachto
asher asah, vayish-bot bayom hash'vee-ee
meekal m'lachto asher asah.
Vay'varech Elohim et yom hash'vee-ee
vay'ka-daysh oto, kee vo shavat meekal m'lachto,
asher barah Elohim la-asot.**

MAGAYN AVOT BIDVARO
("The shield of our forefathers with His word")

This prayer is also called the seven-faceted blessing because it contains references to the Shabbat *Shemoneh Esray* by alluding to its seven blessings. The *Chazan* introduces the prayer with the recital of a blessing similar to the first paragraph of the *Shemoneh Esray.*

The Congregation recites *Magayn Avot*, which is then repeated by the *Chazan*. In some synagogues, *Magayn Avot* is sung by the entire assemblage.

Magayn avot bidvaro,
m'chay-yay maytim b'ma-amaro,
ha-El hakadosh sheh-ayn kamohu,
hamynee-ach l'amo b'yom shabbat kadsho,
kee vam ratzah l'hanee-ach lahem,
l'fanav na-avod b'yirah vafachad,
v'nodeh lishmo b'chal yom tamid,
may-ayn hab'rachot.
El haho-da-ot, adon hashalom,
m'ka-daysh hashabbat oom'varaych sh'vee-ee,
oomaynee-ach bikdushah l'am m'dushnay oneg,
zaycher l'ma-asay v'raysheet.

ELOHAYNU
("Our G-d")

A 348 B 61 BC 275 L 143 DP 81

The final part of this section is recited aloud by the *Chazan*. This is a supplication, exactly the same as the middle blessing in the *Shemoneh Esray*, asking G-d to accept our observance of Shabbat and grant us the many favors we request.

Elohaynu, vaylohay avotaynu,
r'tzay vim'nuchataynu,
kad'shaynu b'mitzvotecha,
v'tayn chel-kaynu b'toratecha,
sab-aynu mee-tuvecha,
v'samchaynu beey'shu-atecha,

v'ta-hayr leebaynu l'avd'cha b'emet.
V'hanchee-laynu Adonai Elohaynu,
b'ahavah uv'ratzon Shabbat kadshecha,
v'yanuchu vah Yisrael m'kadshay sh'mecha.

Baruch ata Adonai, m'kadaysh haShabbat.

℘ KADDISH SHALAYM ℘
("Full *Kaddish*")

A 348 B 61 BC 275 L 143 DP 83

The *Kaddish Shalaym* is the final part of every Congregational service. We praise G-d's name and reiterate our prayer that our service will be accepted. In the Evening Service, the *Kaddish Shalaym* is recited by the *Chazan* prior to the concluding hymns. The Congregation should answer the appropriate responses with great concentration, particularly the phrase, *Amen. Y'hay sh'may rabbah m'varach...* ("May His great name be blessed forever and ever").

Chazan *recites:*
Yitgadal, v'yitkadash, sh'may rabbah. *Cong. responds* Amen.
**B'almah di-v'ra chirutay, v'yamlich malchutay,
b'chayaychon uv'yomaychon, u'v'chayay d'chol
bayt Yisrael, ba-agalah uvizman kareev,
v'imru, Amen.** *Cong. responds* Amen.

Chazan *and Cong. recite together:* **Y'hay sh'may rabbah
m'varach, l'alam ul'almay almahya.**

Chazan *recites:*
**Yitbarach, v'yishtabach, v'yit-pa-ar, v'yit-romam,
v'yit-naseh, v'yit-hadar, v'yit-aleh, v'yit-halal,
sh'may d'kudshah, B'rich Hu.** *Cong. responds* B'rich Hu.

**L'aylah, min kol birchatah v'shiratah,
tush-b'chatah, v'ne-chematah, da-amiran b'almah,
v'imru, Amen.** *Cong. responds* Amen.

**Titkabel tz'lot-hon u-va-ut-hon d'chol bayt Yisrael,
kadam avu-hon di vish-maya,
v'imru, Amen.** *Cong. responds* Amen.

Y'hay sh'lama rabbah min sh'maya, v'chayim,

alaynu v'al kol Yisrael, v'imru, Amen. *Cong. responds* Amen.
Oseh shalom bimro-mav, Hu ya-aseh shalom,
alaynu v'al kol Yisrael, v'imru, Amen. *Cong. responds* Amen.

⚘ CONCLUDING HYMNS ⚘

ALAYNU
("It is our duty")

| A 350 | B 63 | BC 277 | L 143 | DP 87 |

For more than 700 years this has been the final prayer of each of the daily prayers, as well as Festival and Shabbat prayers. In the 9th century, Rabbi Hai Ben David Gaon wrote that this sublime prayer was composed by Joshua as he brought the children of Israel into the Promised Land. Similar to the *Shema*, it declares our faith and expresses our gratitude for being able to serve G-d. Throughout the centuries, *Alaynu* was prohibited or censored in many countries. In particular the line in *Alaynu* stating "they [the other nations] bow to vanity and emptiness..." was considered an attack on other religions and was censored in Europe. In fact, it is still omitted from many prayer books.

Alaynu l'shabayach la-adon hakol, latayt g'dula l'yotzayr b'raysheet. Shelo asanu k'goyay ha-aratzot, v'lo samanu k'mishp'chot ha-adama. Sheh-lo sam chelkaynu kahem,v'goralaynu k'chol hamonam.

(Bow knees and head for the following underlined words.)
<u>Va-anachnu</u> <u>kor'im</u> <u>umishta-chavim</u> umodim, lifnay melech malchay ham'lachim, Hakadosh Baruch Hu.

Shehu noteh shamayim v'yosed aretz, oomashav y'karo bashamayim meema-al, oosh'cheenat oozo b'govhay m'romim, Hu Elohaynu, ayn od. Emet malkaynu, efes zulato, ka-katuv b'torato v'yadata hayom va-hashay-vota el l'vavecha, kee Adonai hu ha-Elohim bashamayim meema-al, v'al ha-aretz meetachat ayn od.

This is the last verse of the second section of Alaynu.
In many synagogues, the Chazan *and Cong. sing this verse together.*

**V'ne-emar, v'haya Adonai, l'melech al kol ha-aretz,
bayom ha-hu yihyeh Adonai echad ush'mo echad.**

❧ KADDISH YATOM ❧
("Mourner's *Kaddish*")

A 352   B 65   BC 279   L 144   DP 91

The Mourner's *Kaddish* is recited at every prayer service for eleven months after the death of a parent. It is also recited on the yearly anniversary *(Yahrtzeit)* of the death. *Kaddish* is a source of merit for the soul. The most important part is the response: *Amen. Y'hay sh'may rabbah m'varach...* ("May His great name be blessed forever and ever.")

Mourner recites:
Yitgadal, v'yitkadash, sh'may rabbah. *Cong. responds* Amen.

**B'almah di-v'ra chirutay, v'yamlich malchutay,
b'chayaychon uv'yomaychon, u'v'chayay d'chol
bayt Yisrael, ba-agalah uvizman kareev,
v'imru, Amen.** *Cong. responds* Amen.

Mourner and Cong. recite together: **Y'hay sh'may rabbah m'varach,
l'alam ul'almay almahya.**

Mourner recites:
**Yitbarach, v'yishtabach, v'yit-pa-ar, v'yit-romam,
v'yit-naseh, v'yit-hadar, v'yit-aleh, v'yit-halal,
sh'may d'kudshah, B'rich Hu.** *Cong. responds* B'rich Hu.

**L'aylah, min kol birchatah v'shiratah,
tushb'chatah, v'ne-chematah, da-amiran b'almah,
v'imru, Amen.** *Cong. responds* Amen.

**Y'hay shlamah rabbah min sh'mayah, v'chayim,
alaynu v'al kol Yisrael, v'imru, Amen.** *Cong. responds* Amen.

**Oseh shalom bimromav, hu ya-aseh shalom,
alaynu v'al kol Yisrael, v'imru, Amen.** *Cong. responds* Amen.

In many Synagogues, the Kiddush *is publicly recited at this point. See page 29 where the* Kiddush *is introduced and transliterated.*

CUSTOMS VARY REGARDING CONCLUDING
HYMNS. SOME SYNAGOGUES RECITE *ADON OLAM,*
OTHERS CONCLUDE THE PRAYER SERVICES WITH *YIGDAL.*

ADON OLAM
("Eternal Lord")

A 352 **B** 67 **BC** 281 **DP** 93

This majestic hymn expresses our absolute trust in G-d's omnipotence and permanence. While *Olam* can mean both eternity and
world, here it is generally understood to refer to the eternity of the
Lord. It is a personal poem exploring the mystery of G-d Who is
both outside the universe and with each and every person.

Adon Olam has been attributed to various medieval poets, and
was most likely written by the Spanish poet Solomon Ibn Gabriol
in the 11th century, although it may date back to Babylonian times.

Cong. and Chazan *sing together.*

**Adon olam asher malach, b'terem kol y'tzir nivrah,
L'ayt na-a-sa b'cheftzo kol, ahzay melech sh'mo nikrah.**

**V'acharay kichlot ha-kol, l'vado yimloch norah,
V'hu haya v'hu hoveh, v'hu yihyeh b'tifarah.**

**V'hu echad, v'ayn shaynee, l'hamsheel lo l'hachbirah,
B'li raysheet, b'li tachlit, v'lo ha-ohz v'hamisrah.**

**V'hu aylee, v'chai go-alee, v'tzur chevlee b'ayt tzarah,
V'hu neesee u-manos lee, m'nat kosee b'yom ekrah.**

**B'yado afkid ruchee, b'ayt eeshan v'ah-eerah,
V'im ruchee g'veeyatee, Adonai lee v'lo eerah.**

YIGDAL
("Exalted")

A 12 **B** 79 **BC** 11 **DP** 95

Yigdal, like *Shema* and *Alaynu,* summarizes the basic Jewish
credo of monotheism. This hymn, consisting of thirteen stanzas, is
based on the great Jewish thinker Maimonides' Thirteen Principles of Faith, (*Ani Maamin*). *Yigdal* seems to have been attributed

to a medieval scholar, Daniel ben Yehuda. Each verse ends in the same rhyme throughout the entire poem.

Cong. and Chazan *sing together:*

**Yigdal Elohim chai, v'yishtabach,
nimtza v'ayn et, el mitzee-uto.**

**Echad v'ayn yachid, k'yee-chudo,
ne-elam v'gam ayn sof, l'achduto.**

**Ayn lo d'mut haguf, v'ayno guf,
lo na-aroch aylav, k'dushato.**

**Kadmon l'chol davar, asher nivra,
reeshon v'ayn raysheet, l'raysheeto.**

**Heeno adon olam, l'chol notzar,
yoreh g'dulato, umalchuto.**

**Shefa n'vu-ato, n'ta-no,
el anshay s'gulato, v'tifarto.**

**Lo kam b'Yisrael, k'Moshe od,
navee umah-beet, et t'munato.**

**Torat emet natan, l'amo El,
al yad n'vee-o, ne-eman bayto.**

**Lo yacha-leef ha-El, v'lo yamir dato,
l'olamim l'zulato.**

**Tzofeh v'yo-day-a, s'taraynu,
mahbeet l'sof davar, b'kadmato.**

**Gomel l'eesh chesed, k'mifalo,
notayn l'rasha ra, k'rish-ato.**

**Yishlach l'kaytz hayamin, m'shee-chaynu,
lifdot m'cha-kay kaytz, y'shu-ato.**

**Maytim y'chayeh El, b'rov chasdo,
baruch aday ad, shem t'heelato.**

THE EVENING PRAYER SERVICES END HERE.

After prayer services it is customary to greet friends or neighbors with *Shabbat Shalom* or *Good Shabbos* and leave the Synagogue in a joyous and happy frame of mind. We look forward to our festive meal and a full day of rest.

One arrives home, to a table set with the wine for *Kiddush* ready and the two *challah* loaves symbolizing the double portion of the Manna covered on the table.

The Talmud (Shab. 119b) teaches that Rabbi Jose, Rabbi Yehuda's son, said, "Two ministering angels accompany one home from Synagogue on the eve of the Shabbat—one a good angel and the other an evil one. When one arrives home and finds the lamp burning, the table set, and the couch covered with a spread, the good angel exclaims, 'May it be thus on another Shabbat too' and the evil angel reluctantly answers '*Amen.*' But if the house is in disarray and nothing is prepared, the evil angel exclaims 'May it be thus on another Shabbat too' and the good angel reluctantly answers '*Amen.*' "

Since these two angels accompany one home from the Synagogue, it is appropriate and fitting to greet the angels and welcome them into our home with the chanting of *Shalom Alaychem*. It is customary to sing each stanza three times.

ঞ SHALOM ALAYCHEM ঞ
("Peace be on you")

A 354 B 67 BC 283 L 144 DP 601

This song is associated with hospitality and finds its source in the above story from the Talmud of visiting angels. It was composed by 17th century Kabbalists. There are varying melodies for this song.

Shalom Alaychem, malachay ha-sha-rayt
Malachay elyon,
Meemelech malchay hamlachim,
HaKadosh Baruch Hu.

Bo-achem l'shalom, malachay hashalom,
Malachay elyon,
Meemelech malchay hamlachim,
HaKadosh Baruch Hu.

Barchunee l'shalom, malachay hashalom,

Malachay elyon,
Meemelech malchay hamlachim,
HaKadosh Baruch Hu.

Tzaytchem l'shalom, malachay hashalom,
Malachay elyon,
Meemelech malchay hamlachim,
HaKadosh Baruch Hu.

Following *Shalom Alaychem*, some people recite the hymn, *Ayshet Chayil* followed by the *Kiddush* and the blessings over the *challahs*. One enjoys a traditional Shabbat dinner which includes the singing of *zemirot* (Shabbat melodies) and the Grace After Meals.

ॐ AYSHET CHAYIL ॐ
("The Woman of Accomplishment")

A 358 BC 287 L 145 DP 601

Ayshet Chayil is an alphabetical acrostic which comes from the concluding twenty-two verses of Proverbs. It was introduced into the *Siddur* by 16th century Kabbalist Rabbi Yitzchak Luria ("The Holy Ari") and his disciples.

On the simplest level, *Ayshet Chayil* honors the woman of the house. How fitting, then, that her husband and children sing this song of praise for her. However, commentators suggest that this poem can also be allegorical and that the passage may refer to the *Shechina* which is G-d's presence in the world, Shabbat, the Torah, the soul, or wisdom. Consequently, in many homes, the entire family sings *Ayshet Chayil* together, so that all may show their love for G-d and His gifts to us.

Ayshet Chayil, mi yimtzah?
v'rachok mipninim michra.
Batach bah lev baalah, v'shalal lo yechsor.
G'malat-hu tov v'lo ra, kol y'may chayeha.
Darsha tzemer ufishtim, vataat b'chayfetz kapeha.
Hoyta k'oniyot socher, meemerchak tavi lachma.
Vatakam b'od layla, vateetayn teref l'vayta

☜ *Blessing the Children* ☞

It is customary to bless one's children, young and old, upon returning home from the Synagogue, prior to reciting the Kiddush.

The standard text of this blessing is:

For a boy:

"Y'simchah Elohim k'Efrayim v'ch'Menasheh."

May G-d make you like Efrayim and Menasheh
(Jacob's grandchildren).

The blessing for a girl is:

"Y'seemaych Elohim k'Sarah, Rivkah, Rachel, v'Leah."

May G-d make you like Sarah, Rivkah, Rachel and Leah
(the four Matriarchs).

These are usually followed by the priestly blessing

"Y'va-rech-che'cha Adonai v'Yish-m'rechah,"

May G-d bless you and keep you,

"Ya-ayr Adonai panav aylechah veey-chu-nekah,"

May G-d shine His countenance on you and favor you.

**"Yeesah Adonai panav aylechah,
v'yasaym l'chah shalom."**

May G-d lift up His countenance on you and give you peace.

The sanctity of the onset of Shabbat makes this a particularly appropriate time to bless one's children. We hope at this auspicious time that we will be blessed to raise our children to study Torah, to marry, and to perform good deeds. We pray, too, that their lives will be dedicated to the service of G-d and that they will merit G-d's blessings for both material and spiritual wealth.

v'chok l'naaroteha.
Zamema sadeh vatee-ka-chayhu,
   mip'ri kapeha nat'ah karem.
Chogra b'oz motneha, vat'amaytz z'ro-oteha.
Ta-ama kee tov sachra, lo yichbeh balayla nayra.
Yadeha shilcha vakeeshor, v'chapeha tomchu falech.
Kapa porsa l'oni, v'yadeha shilcha la-evyon.
Lo teera l'vayta meeshaleg, kee chol vayta lovush shanim.
Marvadim as'ta la, shesh v'argaman l'vusha.
Nodah bash'arim baala, b'shivto im ziknay aretz.
Sadin as'ta vatimkor, vachagor natna lak'naanee.
Oz v'hadar l'vusha, vatis-chak l'yom acharon.
Peeha patcha v'chachma, v'torat chesed al l'shona.
Tzo-feeyah halee-chot bayta, v'lechem atzlut lo tochayl.
Kamu vaneha vay'ashru-ha, baala vay'hal'la.
Rabot banot asoo chayil, v'at aleet al kulana.
Sheker hachayn v'hevel hayofee,
   eesha yirat Adonai—hee tit-halal.
T'nu la mip'ree yadeha,
   vee-hal'luhah bash'arim maa-seha.

❧ KIDDUSH ☙
("Sanctification")

A 360 B 69 BC 289 L 146 DP 83

In the synagogue, the *Chazan* recites the *Kiddush* over a cup of wine in the traditional Shabbat melody. This custom has been retained in most Congregations; however, *Kiddush* should still be recited in one's home prior to the Shabbat meal.

In the Synagogue, the *Chazan* begins the *Kiddush* with the blessing *Baruch atah*....

At home we begin the recital of *Kiddush* with *Vay'chulu*, in order that those members of the family who did not attend Synagogue might hear these Biblical verses, which contain the commandment to rest on the Shabbat.

When reciting *Kiddush* at home, prior to *Vay'chulu*, one should add the words *Vay'hee erev…* and the entire *Kiddush* is recited.

(recited softly) **Vay'hee Erev, vay'hee voker…**

Yom hashee-shee.
Vay'chulu hashamayim v'ha-aretz v'chal tz'va-am.
Vay'chal Elohim bayom hash'vee-ee m'lachto
asher asah, vayish-bot bayom hash'vee-ee
meekal m'lachto asher asah.
Vay'varech Elohim et yom hash'vee-ee
vay'ka-daysh oto, kee vo shavat meekal m'lachto,
asher barah Elohim la-asot.

Savree maranan v'rabanan v'rabotai.
Baruch atah Adonai, Elohaynu melech ha-olam,
boray p'ree hagafen. *Everyone listening responds* Amen.

Baruch atah Adonai, Elohaynu melech ha-olam,
asher kid'shanu b'mitzvotav v'ratzah vanu,
v'Shabbat kadsho, b'ahavah uv'ratzon hin-chee-lanu,
zeekaron l'ma-asay v'ray-sheet.
Kee hu yom t'cheelah l'mikra-ay kodesh,
zaycher leey'tzee-at mitzrayim.
Kee vanu vacharta,
v'otanu keedashta meekol ha-amim,
v'Shabbat kadsh'cha, b'ahavah
uv'ratzon hin-chal-tanu.
Baruch atah Adonai, m'kadaysh haShabbat.

Everyone listening responds Amen.

ॐ AL N'TEELAT YADAYIM ॐ
("Washing the Hands")

Before eating bread we wash our hands.

The washing cup is first held in the left hand and water is poured onto the right hand. The procedure is then reversed. The water should be poured on the entire hand. Customs differ as to how many times each hand should be washed. The general rule is at least twice.

One should not speak between *Al n'teelat yadayim* and *Hamotzi*, except to answer *Amen.*

Baruch atah Adonai,
Elohaynu Melech ha-olam
asher kidshanu b'mitzvotav,
v'tzeevanu al n'teelat yadayim.

HAMOTZEE
("Blessing the Challah")

If the head of the house is reciting the blessing and has in mind that the blessing will fulfill each person's obligation, then the blessing is only recited by the master of the house.

Holding the two challahs *in hand say the following blessing:*
Baruch atah Adonai,
Elohaynu Melech ha-olam
hamotzee lechem min ha-aretz.

FOR A SELECTION OF SHABBAT SONGS, PLEASE SEE PAGE 89.

Outline and Structure of the Shabbat Morning Prayer Service

The Shabbat Morning Prayer Service
is divided into three sections:

1
✺ SHACHARIT ✺
The Morning Service

2
✺ TORAH READING ✺
The Public Reading from the Torah

3
✺ MUSSAF ✺
The Additional Service

Every day of the year we recite the *Shacharit* **Service**. Because of the nature of the Shabbat day, i.e., rest and spiritual meditation, more prayers are inserted into the Shabbat *Shacharit* service than on weekdays.

Every Shabbat the **Torah Reading** of the portion of the week is publicly read so that the entire Five Books will be completed in one year.

The *Mussaf* **Service,** which means additional service, is recited only on special days—Shabbat, *Rosh Chodesh* and Holidays. This Service commemorates the extra sacrifices that were brought on these days when the Great Temple existed in Jerusalem.

— ❦ **4** ❦ —

Shacharit
The Morning Service

hacharit is the Morning Service (the word *Shacharit* comes from the Hebrew word meaning "dawn"). It includes morning blessings, psalms of praise, the *Shema* and *Shemoneh Esray* (silent devotional prayer). It is said that the Morning Service was instituted by Abraham and that the morning prayers reflect Abraham's kind and compassionate nature.

The *Shacharit* Service is arranged in the following order: *Birchot Hashachar*—Morning blessings, *P'sukay D'zimrah*—Psalms of Praise, *The Shema*—Declaration of the Unity of G-d, *Shemoneh Esray*—The Silent Devotion.

❧ BIRCHOT HASHACHAR ❧
("Morning Blessings")

A 12 **B** 75 **BC** 3 **L** 6 **DP** 101

Every morning when we wake up we express our gratitude to G-d, thanking Him for restoring our souls and our strength for another day.

This portion of the service consists of meditation and prayerful thoughts, recited informally in the home or in the synagogue. Several prayers deal with rising in the morning, washing the hands, personal hygiene, and moral and ethical concerns. In these blessings, we thank G-d for the mundane aspects of our lives which are normally taken for granted. Selections from the *Torah* and the *Talmud* recall many of the *Korbanot* ("sacrifices") which were offered to G-d at the time the Temple stood.

⅋ P'SUKAY D'ZIMRAH ⅋
("Psalms of Praise")

After we thank G-d for granting us another day, we praise Him, describing His majesty and glory as the Creator of heaven and earth and the Creator of all living creatures.

This section consists of a beautiful series of chapters mostly from the Psalms (many written by King David), praising G-d's name and His sovereignty, and describing the glory of G-d that surrounds us, as we prepare to say the *Shema* and *Shemoneh Esray*. The Psalms of Praise begin with a blessing, *Baruch She-amar* ("Blessed is He Who spoke") and conclude with a blessing, *Yishtabach* ("May [Your Name] be praised").

Some of the more important prayers in this section are:

BARUCH SHE-AMAR
("Blessed is He Who spoke")

A 370 **B** 119 **BC** 301 **L** 158 **DP** 137

According to tradition, the Rabbis of the Sanhedrin were Divinely inspired when they wrote this poetic introduction to prayer, which blesses seven aspects of G-d.

Cong. and Chazan *recite softly in unison.*

Baruch she-amar v'hayah ha-olam, Baruch hu.
Baruch oseh v'ray-sheet, Baruch omayr v'oseh,
Baruch gozayr um'kayaym, Baruch m'ra-chaym al ha-aretz.
Baruch m'rachaym al habree-yot,
Baruch m'sha-laym sachar tov leey'ray-av,
Baruch chai la-ad, v'kayam la-netzach,

Baruch podeh uma-tzeel, Baruch sh'mo.
Baruch atah Adonai, Elohaynu melech ha-olam,
ha-El, ha-av ha-rachaman, ham'hulal b'feh amo,
m'shu-bach um'fo-ar bilshon chasidav va-avadav,
u'v'shee-ray David av-de-chah,
n'halel-chah Adonai Elohaynu bishvachot, uvizmirot,
n'gadel-chah un'sha-bay-cha-chah, un'fa-er-chah,
v'naz-kir shimchah, v'namlee-ch'chah, malkaynu, Elohaynu.
Yachid chay ha-olamim, melech, m'shubach um'fo-ar,
ah-day ad sh'mo ha-gadol.
Baruch atah Adonai, melech m'hulal batish-ba-chot.

MIZMOR SHIR

("A song [for the *Shabbat*]")

A 388 B 135 BC 317 L 158 DP 155

The *Levites* sang this psalm at the Sabbath Temple Service. It praises G-d and Shabbat and describes the tranquility brought about by our realization of the justice and kindness of G-d's ways.

ASHRAY

("Fortunate")

A 390 B 137 BC 319 L 159 DP 159

This prayer (Psalm 145) contains most of the letters of the aleph-bet which symbolizes that we praise G-d with everything at our disposal and that G-d takes care of each and every form of life. *Ashray* signifies good fortune and affirms how fortunate we feel to dwell in G-d's house. The psalm extols G-d's virtues and His intimate involvement in the world. The Rabbis of the Talmud declared that those who recite this psalm three times daily will be assured a share in the World to Come.

NISHMAT

("The soul [of every living thing]")

A 400 B 149 BC 331 L 165 DP 173

Our complete dependency on G-d is described in this moving

and beautiful prayer. We again express praise and gratitude to G-d for all the myriads of things He has done for us. In this outpouring of praise we exclaim, "Were our mouths as full of song as the sea is of water and our tongues as full of joyous song as its multitude of waves..."

SHO-CHAYN-AD
("He Who lives forever")

A 404 **B** 151 **BC** 333 **L** 168 **DP** 175

The *Chazan* begins the *Shacharit* Service here in the special *Shabbat* melody.

Sho-chayn ad marom v'kadosh sh'mo.
V'chatoov ran'noo tzadikim baAdonai,
la-y'sharim na-ava t'heellah.

B'fee y'sharim tit-halal,
oov'divray tzadikim titba-rach,
oovilshon chassidim tit-ro-mam,
oov'kerev k'doshim tit-ka-dash

YISHTABACH
("May Your Name be praised")

A 404 **B** 153 **BC** 335 **L** 169 **DP** 177

This concluding blessing of the Psalms of Praise contains fifteen praises of G-d and declares that as much as we have lauded G-d, He is, in fact, far greater than can ever be described.

The Congregation rises and, together with the Chazan, *recites this softly.*
Yishtabach shimchah la-ad malkaynu,
ha-el hamelech hagadol v'hakadosh,
bashamayim, uva-aretz.
Kee l'chah na-eh Adonai Elohaynu, vaylohay
avotaynu, shir ush'vacha, hallel v'zimrah,
oz umemshalah, netzach, g'dulah ug'vurah,
t'heelah v'tiferet, k'dushah umalchut,
B'rachot, v'hoda-ot, may-atah v'ad olam.

**Baruch atah Adonai, El, melech, gadol
batish-bachot, El hahoda-ot, adon hanifla-ot,
habo-chayr b'sheeray zimrah,
melech, El, chay ha-olamim.**

☞ THE HALF KADDISH ☜

A 406 B 153 BC 335 L 42 DP 177

In this ancient prayer we ask that G-d's name be exalted throughout the world. The Congregation should recite the appropriate responses with concentration and devotion, especially *Amen, Y'hay sh'may rabbah m'varach...* ("May His great name be blessed forever and ever").

Chazan recites:
Yitgadal, v'yitkadash, sh'may rabbah. *Cong. responds* Amen.
**B'almah di-v'ra chirutay, v'yamlich malchutay,
b'chayaychon uv'yomaychon, u'v'chayay d'chol
bayt Yisrael, ba-agalah uvizman kareev,
v'imru, Amen.** *Cong. responds* Amen.

Chazan and Cong. recite together: **Y'hay sh'may rabbah
m'varach, l'alam ul'almay almahyah.**

**Yitbarach, v'yishtabach, v'yit-pa-ar, v'yit-romam,
v'yit-naseh, v'yit-hadar, v'yit-aleh, v'yit-halal,
sh'may d'kudshah, B'rich Hu.** *Cong. responds* B'rich Hu.

**L'aylah, min kol birchatah v'shiratah,
tushb'chatah, v'ne-chematah, da-amiran b'almah,
v'imru, Amen.** *Cong. responds* Amen.

☞ BARCHU ☜
(Invitation to Congregation to bless G-d)

A 406 B 153 BC 335 L 170 DP 179

The *Chazan* summons the Congregation to bless G-d, which is followed by the Congregational response.

The Chazan *and Cong. bow slightly at the command* Barchu *and everyone stands erect when G-d's name is recited.*

Chazan **Barchu Et Adonai Ham-vorach**

Everyone again bows at the word Baruch *and straightens up at G-d's name.*

Cong. **Baruch Adonai Ham-vorach L'olam Va-ed**

This sentence is repeated by the Chazan.

ॐ THE SHEMA AND ITS BLESSINGS ᛕ

The *Shema* affirms the Oneness of G-d and our acceptance of all His commandments. Because we are inspired by G-d's goodness and love, after thanking Him and praising Him, we now declare His absolute sovereignty, and accept upon ourselves the commitment to observe His commandments.

Following *Barchu* we will recite two blessings that precede the *Shema*: *Yotzayr Ohr* ("Who Creates the Luminaries") and *Ahavah Rabbah* ("[with] abundant love"). Included in the first blessing is the lovely hymn *El Adon (G-d the Master)*, which is an alphabetical arrangement of praise and glory to G-d—Creator of all the heavenly bodies.

EL ADON
("G-d, the Master")

A 410 **B** 157 **BC** 339 **L** 171 **DP** 181

This alphabetically arranged poem praises G-d's greatness, with special emphasis on the heavenly bodies.

Chazan and Cong. recite or sing together.

El Adon al kol ha-ma-asim,
Baruch um'vorach b'fee kol n'shamah,
Gadlo u'vtuvo maleh olam,
Da-at ut'vunah sov'vim oto.

Hamitgah-eh al chayot hakodesh,
V'ne-he-dar b'chavod al hamerkavah,
Z'chut umeeshor lifnay chis-oh,
Chesed v'rachamim lifnay ch'vodo.

Tovim m'o-rot she-barah Elohaynu,
Y'tzaram b'da-at b'veenah u'v'haskayl,
Ko-ach ug'vurah natan bahem,
Lihyot moshlim b'kerev tayvayl.

M'layim ziv oom'feekim nogah,
Na-eh zeevam b'chol ha-olam,
S'maychim b'tzaytam v'sasim b'vo-am,
Osim b'aymah r'tzon konam.

P'er v'chavod notnim lishmo,
Tzahalah v'reenah l'zaycher malchuto,
Karah la-shemesh vayizrach ohr,
Ra-ah v'hitkin tzurat hal'vanah.

She-vach notnim lo,
Kol tz'vah mahrom,
Tiferet ug'dulah,
S'rafim v'ofanim v'chayot hakodesh.

ℐ KEDUSHAH ℘

A 412 B 159 BC 341 L 174 DP 185

Following the praises of G-d as the Creator of all things, we recite the Modified *Kedushah*, the song in which the angels
proclaim the holiness of G-d.

Cong. and Chazan *in unison.*

Kadosh, Kadosh, Kadosh, Adonai Tz'va-ot, Meloh Chol Ha-aretz K'vodo.

("Holy, Holy, Holy is the G-d of hosts; the whole
earth is full of His glory.")

Cong. and Chazan *in unison.*

Baruch K'vod Adonai Mimkomo.

("Blessed is the glory of G-d from His place")

ℐ BLESSINGS OF THE SHEMA ℘

The first blessing of Shema, *Yotzayr Ohr* ("Who Creates the
Luminaries") is lengthy and praises G-d for creating the heavenly
bodies and the angels. It concludes with the words *Yotzayr
Ham'orot* ("Who creates the Luminaries"), after which the
Congregation responds *Amen.*

Ahavah Rabbah ("[with] abundant love") is the second
blessing, and it is said just prior to reciting the *Shema.* In this
blessing we thank G-d for the Torah and pray for the wisdom to

understand and observe it. We also plead that G-d will gather the Jews from everywhere on earth and return us to our Holy Land. It concludes with the words *Habo-chayr B'amo Yisrael B'ahavah* ("Who chooses His people Israel with love"), after which the Congregation responds *Amen*.

THE SHEMA
(Acceptance of G-d's sovereignty)

A 414 B 161 BC 343 L 175 DP 187

The first passage of the *Shema* (from Deuteronomy 6:4) and the three paragraphs that follow are part of both the daily morning and evening worship services. The *Shema* is the most important single sentence in the liturgy, for in it we affirm that G-d is One.

It is the Jew's confession of faith and many martyrs have died with this prayer on their lips. The *Shema* is so important and so well summarizes the basic tenets of Judaism that its first two paragraphs are inscribed on the scrolls of both the *mezuzah* and *tefillin*.

It is important to concentrate fully on all three paragraphs, because the recitation of the *Shema* represents the acceptance of G-d's absolute sovereignty.

For men wearing a *Tallit*, the four corners are gathered together prior to the recital of the *Shema* and held in the left hand between one's last two fingers. At the mention of the word *tzitzit* in the final paragraph, the *tzitzit* are moved to the right hand and kissed. At the last word of the *Shema*—*Emet*, the *t*zitzit are again kissed. *(For additional explanation, please refer to pages 11-15.)*

SHEMA YISRAEL
("Hear O Israel")

Chazan *and Cong. recite aloud, carefully enunciating each word.*
Shema Yisrael, Adonai Elohaynu, Adonai Echad
("Hear O Israel, The Lord is our G-d, The Lord is One")

Chazan *and Cong. recite in an undertone.*
Baruch Shem K'vod Malchuto L'olam Va-ed
("Blessed be the name of the glory of His Kingdom forever and ever")

The following three paragraphs are said softly to oneself. The first paragraph, *V'ahavta*, addressed to us as individuals, concentrates on how we shall love G-d with all our heart. The second paragraph, *V'haya*, addressed to us as a nation, affirms our acceptance of all of G-d's commandments and belief in reward and punishment. The third paragraph, *Vayomer*, discusses *tzitzit* and the Exodus from Egypt.

V'AHAVTA
("And you shall love")

Cong. recites softly to themselves.

V'ahavta et Adonai Elohecha, b'chol l'vav'cha, uv'chol nafsh'cha, uv'chol m'odecha. V'hayu had'varim ha-ayleh, asher anochee m'tzav'cha hayom, al l'vavecha. V'sheenantam l'vanecha, v'deebarta bam, b'shivt'cha b'vaytecha, uv'lecht'cha vaderech, uv'shochb'cha uv'kumecha.
Uk'shartam l'ot al yadecha, v'hayu l'totafot bayn aynecha. Uch'tavtam al m'zuzot baytecha, uvish'arecha.

V'HAYA
("And it will come to pass")

Cong. recites softly to themselves.

V'haya im sha-moah tishm'u el mitzvotai, asher anochee m'tzaveh et-chem hayom, l'ahavah et Adonai Elohaychem ul'avdo, b'chol l'vavchem uv'chol nafsh'chem. V'natati m'tar artz'chem b'eeto, yoreh umalkosh, v'asafta d'ganecha, v'teerosh'cha v'yitz-harecha. V'natati aysev b'sadcha livhemtecha, v'achalta v'savata. Heeshamru lachem, pen yifteh l'vavchem, v'sartem va-avad'tem elohim achayrim, v'hishtachaveetem lahem. V'chara af Adonai bachem, v'atzar et hashamayim, v'lo yihyeh matar, v'ha-adamah lo teetayn et y'vulah, va-avadtem m'hayrah, may-al ha-aretz hatovah, asher Adonai notayn lachem. V'samtem et d'varai ayleh, al l'vavchem v'al nafsh'chem, uk'shartem otam l'ot al yedchem, v'hayu l'totafot bayn aynaychem. V'leemad'tem otam et b'naychem,

☙ *The Shema—Baruch Shem K'vod Malchuto* ☙

hen Jacob, who was also called Israel, was about to die, he wanted to reveal to his children what would happen at the end of time, but the Divine Presence was taken away from him. Not knowing why the Divine Presence was withheld, he feared that perhaps there was a taint of idolatry in his children and that perhaps they did not believe that G-d was One and His Name One.

He asked them and they answered, "Hear O Israel, the Lord is our G-d, the Lord is One."

At that time, Jacob praised and thanked G-d and said, "Blessed be the Name of the glory of His Kingdom, forever and ever."

Our Sages comment that we should recite the *Shema* out loud since the *Shema* is written in the Torah, but since *Baruch Shem K'vod...* was not, we recite it in an undertone.

Others say that when Moses went on High to receive the tablets of the Law, he heard the angels praising G-d, saying, "Blessed be the Name..." and transmitted this sentence to the Israelites. Since it is an angelic prayer, we recite it silently during the year and only recite it aloud on Yom Kippur, when we are all likened to angels.

l'dabayr bam, b'shivt'cha b'vaytecha,
uv'lecht'cha vaderech, uv'shochb'cha uv'kumecha.
Uch'tavtam al m'zuzot baytecha, uvish'arecha.
L'ma-an yirbu y'maychem, veeymay v'naychem
al ha-adamah asher nishba Adonai la-avotaychem
latayt lahem, keeymay hashamayim al ha-aretz.

VAYOMER
("And G-d said")

Cong. recites softly to themselves.

Vayomer Adonai el Moshe laymor. Dabayr el B'nay
Yisrael, v'amarta alayhem, v'asu lahem tzitzit,
al kanfay vigdayhem l'dorotam, v'natnu al tzitzit
hakanaf p'til t'chaylet. V'haya lachem l'tzitzit,
ur'eetem oto, uz'chartem et kol mitzvot Adonai,
va-aseetem otam. V'lo taturu acharay l'vavchem,
v'acharay aynaychem asher atem zonim acharayhem.
L'ma-an tizk'ru, va-aseetem et kol mitzvotai, v'heyeetem
k'doshim laylohaychem. Ani Adonai Elohaychem,
asher hotzaytee etchem may-eretz Mitzrayim, lihyot
lachem laylohim, Ani

Make sure these final three words are said without interruption:

Adonai Elohaychem, emet.

CONCLUDING BLESSING OF THE SHEMA

As we prepare for the Silent Devotion, we recite several additional prayers, including the final blessing, *Ga-al Yisrael*, which elaborates on the exodus from Egypt and concludes with a plea that G-d manifest himself again and redeem Israel from exile.

The Cong. rises in preparation for the Shemoneh Esray, *the Silent Devotion.*

MI CHAMOCHAH
("Who is like You")

A 418 B 167 **BC** 349 **L** 178 **DP** 193

Mee chamochah ba-aylim Adonai,
mee kamochah ne-edar bakodesh,

norah t'heelot o-say feleh.

ADONAI YIMLOCH
("God will reign")

A 418 **B** 167 **BC** 349 **L** 178 **DP** 193

Adonai Yimloch L'olam Va-ed.
Tzur Yisrael, kumah b'ezrat Yisrael,
oof'day chinu-mechah Yehudah v'Yisrael.
Go-alaynu Adonai tz'va-ot sh'mo k'dosh Yisrael.
Baruch atah Adonai, Ga-al Yisrael.

֍ SHEMONEH ESRAY ֍
(Silent Devotion)

A 420 **B** 167 **BC** 349 **L** 178 **DP** 195

The *Amidah* or *Shemoneh Esray* is the central part of the Morning Service. *Amidah*, another name for this prayer, means "standing," after the position one must take while saying it. *Shemoneh Esray* means "eighteen," which is the number of blessings originally included in the Silent Devotion of the weekday service. The name *Shemoneh Esray* has been retained as the name for all the silent devotional prayers, even though on Shabbat and holidays the Silent Devotion contains only seven blessings.

The *Shemoneh Esray* is the only prayer recited at every single daily and holiday synagogue service throughout the year. Its seven Shabbat and holiday benedictions and nineteen weekday blessings embrace the three dimensions necessary for Jewish prayer: Praise, Petition and Thanksgiving. The blessings of praise and thanksgiving are the same every day of the year, but on Shabbat and holidays, the weekday benedictions of petition are reduced from thirteen to one because on these special days, our personal needs are provided for and thus there is no need for more petitions.

The following is a summary of the three sections of the *Shemoneh Esray*:

Praise—The first of the three blessings recognizes the glory of G-d. We approach G-d as children of Abraham, Isaac and Jacob, with whom He made an eternal covenant. We come to G-d, who is kind, supports the fallen, heals the sick and eventually restores life to the dead. G-d is holy and we, His children, recognize His omniscience.

Petition—The middle blessing expresses the holiness of the day. This section contains several paragraphs relating to the Shabbat including the Biblical narrative of the Seventh day and a request that G-d sanctify the Shabbat for us as an eternal heritage.

Thanksgiving—Having concluded our requests, we can now close the *Amidah* with three blessings expressing our gratitude. This is similar to a petitioner withdrawing from a king's royal presence. This section includes a prayer for peace and prayer where we ask for G-d's protection.

ℳ CHAZARAT HASHATZ ℵ
("*Chazan*'s Repetition")

Following the Silent Devotion, Congregational prayer includes, at this point, the *Chazan's* repetition of the *Shemoneh Esray* with the recital of *Kedushah*. It is most important for the congregation to intently follow the repetition and refrain from speaking.

ℳ KEDUSHAH ℵ
(Sanctification of G-d's Name)

A 422 B 169 BC 351 L 179 DP 197

The Children of Israel join the angels in praising G-d in this most significant part of the *Chazan's* repetition which is the sanctification of G-d's name in the highest heavens. In *Ezekiel* we find that the angels who surround G-d keep their feet together when going before G-d. We do the same for this prayer.

N'kadaysh et shimchah ba-olam,
k'shaym sheh-makdeeshim oto, bishmay marom,
ka-katuv al yad n'vee-echah,
v'karah zeh el zeh, v'amar

Cong. and Chazan *together. During the first three words we rise on our toes.*
Kadosh, Kadosh, Kadosh, Adonai Tz'va-ot

Meloh Chol Ha-aretz K'vodo.

Cong. recites, Chazan *repeats.*

Az b'kol, ra-ash gadol, adir v'chazak, mashmee-im kol, mit-nasim l'umat serafim, l'umatam baruch yomayru.

Cong. and Chazan *together. During the word* Baruch *we rise on our toes.*

Baruch K'vod Adonai Mimkomo.

Cong. recites, Chazan *repeats.*

**Mimkomcha malkaynu toh-fee-ah,
v'timloch alaynu, ki m'chakim anachnu lach.
Matai timloch b'tziyon,
b'karov, b'yamaynu, l'olam va-ed tishkon.
Titgadal, v'titkadash, b'toch Yerushalayim irchah,
l'dor vador, ul'naytzach n'tzachim.
V'aynaynu tir-ehnah, malchu-techah,
kadavar ha-amur b'sheeray uzechah.
Al y'day David, m'shee-ach tzidkechah.**

Cong. and Chazan *together. During the word* Yimloch *we rise on our toes.*

**Yimloch Adonai L'olam, Elohayich Tziyon,
L'dor Vador, Halleluyah.**

THE *CHAZAN*'S REPETITION CONTINUES.
AT THE *MODIM* PRAYER WE RISE AND BOW AT THE
WORD *MODIM* AS THE CHAZAN RECITES *MODIM* ALOUD.

✲ KADDISH SHALAYM ✲
("Full *Kaddish*")

The full *Kaddish* is the final part of every service. We praise G-d's name and reiterate our prayer that our service will be accepted. The Congregation should answer the appropriate responses with great concentration, particularly the phrase, *Amen, Y'hay sh'may rabbah m'varach...* ("May His great name be blessed forever and ever").

Chazan recites.

Yitgadal, v'yitkadash, sh'may rabbah. *Cong. responds* Amen.
**B'almah di-v'ra chirutay, v'yamlich malchutay,
b'chayaychon uv'yomaychon, u'v'chayay d'chol
bayt Yisrael, ba-agalah uvizman kareev,
v'imru, Amen.** *Cong. responds* Amen.

Chazan *and Cong. recite together:* **Y'hay sh'may rabbah m'varach, l'alam ul'almay almahya.**

Chazan recites.

Yitbarach, v'yishtabach, v'yit-pa-ar, v'yit-romam, v'yit-naseh, v'yit-hadar, v'yit-aleh, v'yit-halal, sh'may d'kudshah, B'rich Hu. *Cong. responds* B'rich Hu.

L'aylah, min kol birchatah v'shiratah, tush-b'chatah, v'ne-chematah, da-amiran b'almah, v'imru, Amen. *Cong. responds* Amen.

Titkabel tz'lot-hon u-va-ut-hon d'chol bayt Yisrael, kadam avu-hon di vish-maya, v'imru, Amen. *Cong. responds* Amen.

Y'hay sh'lama rabbah min sh'maya, v'chayim, alaynu v'al kol Yisrael, v'imru, Amen. *Cong. responds* Amen.

Oseh shalom bimro-mav, Hu ya-aseh shalom, alaynu v'al kol Yisrael, v'imru, Amen. *Cong. responds* Amen.

ℐ CONCLUSION ℕ

If the *Shabbat* coincides with *Chanukah*, a Festival, or *Rosh Chodesh*, the *Hallel* is recited before the *Kaddish Shalaym* (*see page 49*).

In some Congregations, the Rabbi discusses the weekly Bible portion at this point. Where there is no interruption, the Torah will be removed from the *Aron* for the weekly reading.

✹ Joseph Honors the Shabbat ✹

The Talmud (Shab. 119a) relates the story of the great reward that came to a man who honored the Shabbat. There once was a poor Jewish man who worked for a gentile, an owner of much property and an unkind man. The Jew was harshly treated by his boss and lived a life of poverty, except when it came to honoring the Shabbat. During the weekdays, he sustained his family on meager rations, but when the Shabbat came, he dressed in his finest clothing and ate choice dishes of fish and meat.

Accordingly, he was called by the Jewish townspeople, "Joseph who honored the Shabbat."

Once the gentile man had a dream and was told that "all the property you have came to you through Joseph and to him they shall return." Fearful of the dream, the gentile man decided to sell all his property and all his possessions, with which he bought a precious stone. He hid the stone in his turban, saying to himself, "Now let's see Joseph get my wealth."

Not long after, the gentile was crossing a bridge and the wind blew the turban off his head and into the sea. The man became hysterical and went below to the water to try and save it but the water was rough and he couldn't reach the turban.

The precious stone eventually fell out of the turban and a fish swallowed the stone. Soon the fish was caught by a fisherman and the fish was brought to the market on *erev* Shabbat. The fisherman tried his best to sell it but no one bought it. It was late and the fisherman, eager to sell his catch, was told to take it to Joseph, who would buy it. Sure enough, Joseph purchased the fish, and while preparing it for the Shabbat, was amazed to find a precious gem, more dazzling than any he had ever seen before. Greatly rejoicing and thanking God, after the Shabbat, he sold the stone and became a wealthy man.

5

Hallel
Hymns of Praise

ur sages ordained the recital of *Hallel* on *Rosh Chodesh*, *Chanukah* and Festivals to express our joy and also to commemorate deliverance of our nation from peril. *Hallel*—which in Hebrew means "praise"—basically contains six heartfelt and exuberant psalms of praise that were composed by King David. Other verses are included in the *Hallel* because they highlight important events in Jewish history: The Exodus, the splitting of the sea, the giving of the *Torah*, the future resurrection of the dead and the coming of the Messiah.

The *Hallel*'s mood is celebratory. We express how grateful we are that—"This is the day which the Lord made, let us exult and rejoice on it."

On *Rosh Chodesh* and the last six days of *Pesach*, an abridged version of *Hallel* is recited, commonly known as Half *Hallel*, since two paragraphs, *Lo Lanu* and *Ahavti*, are omitted.

The *Hallel* begins with a *bracha* (blessing) and ends with a *bracha*. We have included a selection of hymns from the *Hallel*.

Hallel is said while standing because it is considered that by saying *Hallel* we are testifying to G-d's power.

☙ THE INTRODUCTORY BLESSING ❧

A 632 **B** 339 **BC** 565 **L** 241 **DP** 221

Chazan recites, Cong. repeats.

Baruch atah Adonai, Elohaynu Melech ha-olam, asher kidshanu b'mitzvotav, v'tzeevanu likroh et haHallel.

☙ B'TZAYT YISRAEL ❧
("When Israel went out")

A 632 **B** 341 **BC** 567 **L** 242 **DP** 221

This lilting hymn is Psalm 114 and recounts the Jews' departure and liberation from Egypt.

**B'tzayt Yisrael mee-mitzrayim,
bayt Yaakov may-am loez,
hoytah Yehuda l'kadsho, Yisrael mamshelotav.**

**Hayam ra-ah vayanos,
ha-yardayn yeesov l'achor,
heh-harim rakdu ch'aylim, g'va-ot kivnay tzon.**

**Mah l'chah hayam, kee tanus,
hayardayn teesov l'achor,
heh-harim tirk'du ch'aylim, g'va-ot kivnay tzon.**

**Meelifnay Adon chulee aretz,
meelifnay Elo-ah Yaakov,
ha-hofchee hatzur agam mahyim,
chalamish l'maino mahyim.**

☙ Y'VARAYCH ❧
("He will bless")

A 634 **B** 343 **BC** 569 **L** 242 **DP** 223

Here we bless G-d for all He has bestowed upon us at all times. This excerpt is from Psalm 115.

Adonai, z'charanu y'vahraych.

Y'vahraych et bayt Yisrael,
y'vahraych et bayt Aharon,
y'vahraych yiray Adonai,
ha-k'tanim im hag'dolim.

Yosayf Adonay alaychem,
alaychem v'al b'naychem,
b'ruchim atem laAdonai,
oseh shamayim va-aretz.

Hashmayim shamayim laAdonai,
v'ha-aretz natan livnay adam.

Lo ha-maytim y'ha-l'lu Yah,
v'lo kol yorday dumah.

Va-anachnu n'va-raych yah,
may-atah v'ad olam, Halleluyah.

☙ HAL'LU ☙
("Praise")

A 638 **B** 345 **BC** 571 **L** 243 **DP** 227

There are many different melodies for this joyous verse from Psalm 117—"Praise the Lord, all nations, laud Him, all peoples. For His kindness has overwhelmed us, and the truth of the Lord is eternal. Halleluyah." Often the Congregation and then *Chazan* say this aloud.

Hal'lu et Adonai, kol goyim,
shab'chuhu kol ha-umim,
ki gavar alaynu chasdo,
v'emet Adonai l'olam, Halleluyah.

☙ HODU ☙
("Give thanks")

A 638 **B** 345 **BC** 571 **L** 243 **DP** 227

This hymn (Psalm 118) to G-d's kindness is recited aloud by the *Chazan* and repeated by the Congregation.

Hodu laAdonai ki tov,   ki l'olam chasdo.
Yomar na Yisrael,   ki l'olam chasdo.
Yomru na vayt Aharon, ki l'olam chasdo.
Yomru na yiray Adonai, ki l'olam chasdo.

🕊 ODECHA 🕊
("I thank You")

A 640   B 347   BC 573   L 244   DP 229

Another joyous song from Psalm 118. Each of the verses is repeated twice. The English translation is as follows: "I shall thank You because You answered me, and You were my salvation. The stone that builders rejected became a cornerstone. This was from the Lord; it is wondrous in our eyes. This is the day that the Lord made; let us rejoice and be glad on it."

Odecha ki aneeta-nee, vat-hi lee leey'shuah.
Odecha ki aneeta-nee, vat-hi lee leey'shuah.

Even ma-asu habonim, hoytah l'rosh peenah.
Even ma-asu habonim, hoytah l'rosh peenah.

May-ayt Adonai hoytah zot, hee niflat b'aynaynu.
May-ayt Adonai hoytah zot, hee niflat b'aynaynu.

Zeh hayom asah Adonai, nageelah v'nism'chah vo.
Zeh hayom asah Adonai, nageelah v'nism'chah vo.

🕊 ANAH ADONAI 🕊
("Please G-d")

A 640   B 347   BC 573   L 244   DP 231

This is a famous plea to G-d to save and make prosperous all who come to take shelter in G-d's shade and return to His worship.

Chazan *recites, Cong. repeats each verse.*
Anah Adonai ho-shee-ah na.

Anah Adonai ho-shee-ah na.

Anah Adonai hatzleechah na.

Anah Adonai hatzleechah na.

Kriyat Hatorah
The Torah Reading

etween *Shacharit*, (the Morning Service) and *Mussaf* ("Additional Service") we read from the Torah. A Torah scroll is the result of an exacting labor of love by a dedicated and specially trained scribe. For thousands of years the Hebrew calligraphy used to write these scrolls has been the same. There are laws regarding every detail of the scroll, from the preparation of the parchment (made from the hide of a kosher animal) to the ink and the shape of the letters. No vocalization, punctuation or musical notes appear in the text. The sexton of the synagogue or a trained layman reads the text following a cantillation method that has remained unchanged for more than two millennia.

The Torah is divided into 54 portions. Each year the cycle of reading in all synagogues is both completed and begun on the holiday of *Simchat Torah*. The weekly portion is called the *sedra* or *parsha*, and the name of each week's *sedra* usually comes from the first word of that portion. Because of the nature of the calendar, two *sedrot* are read together in certain weeks, in order to complete the cycle at the appropriate time. On holidays, portions from the

Torah pertaining to the specific holiday are read.

The Torah scroll is dressed and decorated in a style reflecting the priestly dress of Temple times. A breastplate, robe and belt were all worn by the High Priest in Jerusalem. Since the destruction of the Temple in 70 C.E., we use the ancient symbols of priesthood to preserve a link with the past. The robe, mantle and belt of the Torah scroll are usually made of the finest materials — velvet or silk magnificently embroidered by hand, with the breastplate made of ornate silver.

Males over the age of thirteen are involved in the Torah service by means of an *Aliyah* (literally, "Ascent"). This is an honor given to those who recite the blessings of the Torah. It is called *Aliyah* for two reasons. First one must literally ascend to the synagogue's elevated *bimah* ("platform"). Second, reading from the Torah in front of the Congregation is considered such an honor that it is also a moment of spiritual ascent.

The first *Aliyah* is given to a *Kohayn*, the second to a *Levi* and the third and all subsequent *Aliyot* to *Yisraelim*. This order accords honor to the priests who performed the service in the Temple and also to the *Levites* who supervised the maintenance of the ancient Temple and its sacred rituals. It also forestalls any rivalry that might arise from everyone clamoring for the first *Aliyah*.

⍀ ORDER OF THE TORAH SERVICE ℣
REMOVAL OF THE TORAH FROM THE ARON

The service continues with a series of introductory verses celebrating the greatness and majesty of G-d and expressing our desire for Jerusalem to be rebuilt. When the *Aron* is opened, we rise and declare the invincibility of G-d's word.

AV HARACHAMIM
("Father of Compassion")

A 432 **B** 181 **BC** 363 **L** 185 **DP** 237

Chazan *and Cong. recite or sing in unison.*

Av harachamim, hayteevah virtzoncha, et tziyon.
Tivneh chomot Yerushalayim.
Ki v'cha l'vad batach-nu,

melech El ram v'neesah, Adon olamim.

The Aron is opened.

VAY'HEE BINSO-AH

("And it came to pass that when the *Aron* would travel")

A 432 B 181 BC 363 L 183 DP 237

These few verses allude to the fact that when the *Aron* in the desert was to travel, Moses implored God to rise up and the enemies of the Jews will be vanquished. It is therefore an appropriate prayer to be recited when the *Aron* is opened for the removal of the Torah.

Chazan and Cong. sing in unison.

Vay'hee binso-ah ha-aron, vayomer Moshe.
Kumah Adonai, v'yafutzu oyvechah,
v'yanusu m'sanecha mee-panecha.
Kee mee-tziyon taytzay Torah,
u'dvar Adonai mee-Y-rushalayim.
Baruch she-natan, Torah,
l'amo Yisrael bikdushato.

BEH ANA RACHITZ

("In Him I put my trust")

A 436 B 183 BC 365 L 184 DP 241

These are the concluding lines of *Brich Sh'may* ("Blessed is the Name"), a prayer written in Aramaic, depicting G-d's mercy, praising Him and extolling His goodness on behalf of the people of Israel. In the second century Rabbi Simeon stated that "when the Torah is removed to be read, the gates of mercy in heaven are opened and the attribute of G-d's love is stirred up."

Chazan and Cong. recite or sing in unison.

Beh, ana rachitz.
V'lishmay kadeeshah, yakeerah,
ana aymar tushb'chan.

Y'hay rabbah kadamach,
d'tiftach liba-ee b'o-raytah,

**v'tashlim misha-lin d'leeba-ee,
v'leebah d'chal amach, Yisrael,
l'tav ul'chayin, v'lishlam, Amen.**

The Torah Scroll is removed, the Aron *is closed and the* Chazan *and Congregation responsively chant* Shema Yisrael *and* Echad Elohaynu. *The third sentence,* Gadlu, *is recited by the* Chazan *alone.*

◈ SHEMA YISRAEL ◈
("Hear O Israel")

A 436 **B** 183 **BC** 365 **L** 185 **DP** 241

**Shema Yisrael, Adonai Elohaynu, Adonai Echad.
Echad Elohaynu, Gadol Adonaynu, Kadosh Sh'mo.
Gadlu LaAdonai Eetee, Un'romemah Sh'mo Yachdav.**

We pay homage to the Torah now as the scroll is escorted through the Congregation. While the Torah is carried around the synagogue to the Bimah, *the hymn* L'chah Adonai *is sung.*

L'CHAH ADONAI
("To You, G-d")

A 436 **B** 183 **BC** 365 **L** 185 **DP** 241

**L'chah Adonai hag'dulah, v'hag'vurah,
v'hatiferet, v'hanaytzach, v'ha-hod,
ki chol bashamayim uva-aretz.
L'chah Adonai hamamlachah v'hamitna-seh
l'chol l'rosh. Rom'mu Adonai Elohaynu, v'hishtachavu
lahadom raglav kadosh hu. Rom'mu Adonai Elohaynu,
v'hishtachavu l'har kadsho, kee kadosh Adonai Elohaynu.**

◈ READING OF THE BIBLE PORTION ◈

The weekly section of the Bible is publicly read. In a regular Synagogue setting, at least seven men are called upon to recite the blessings in praise of the Torah and the Torah Portion is read in its own special musical cantillation. There will be certain occasions during the year, when more than one Torah will be removed i.e., *Rosh Chodesh.*

BLESSINGS OF THE TORAH

If given the honor to recite the blessings, the Ba-al Koreh *(one who reads the Torah) will show you the place where the reading commences. Take the corner of your* Tallit, *touch the place where the reading will begin, and kiss the* tzitzit. *Then recite the following blessing aloud, bowing at* Barchu *and straightening up at* Adonai.

Reader of blessings recites.
Barchu et Adonai Ham-vorach.

Cong. responds, Reader of blessings repeats.
Baruch Adonai Ham-vorach l'olam va-ed.

Reader of blessings recites.
**Baruch atah Adonai, Elohaynu melech ha-olam,
asher ba-char banu, meekol ha-amim,
v'na-tan la-nu et torato.
Baruch atah Adonai, notayn haTorah.** *Cong. responds* Amen.

At the conclusion of the reading, take the corner of your Tallit, *touch the place where the reading has just ended, kiss the* tzitzit *and recite the following blessing aloud.*

Reader of blessings recites.
**Baruch atah Adonai, Elohaynu melech ha-olam,
asher na-tan lanu torat emet,
v'cha-yay olam nata b'tochaynu.
Baruch atah Adonai, notayn haTorah.** *Cong. responds* Amen.

Prior to the lifting of the Torah, it is appropriate to publicly recite a prayer for the sick included in the Siddur. *In some Synagogues, the entire Congregation recites the prayer together. In others, the Rabbi or Sexton recites the prayer aloud, and the names of the sick are inserted in the appropriate place.*

At the conclusion of the Torah reading, the Half *Kaddish* is recited and two people are called, one to lift and the other to tie the Torah. The one who lifts the Torah is called the *Magbeah* and the one who ties it is called the *Gollel.* The purpose of raising the Torah is to show that the Torah is an open book and belongs to all the people. When the Torah is lifted, the Congregation rises and chants:

⍥ King David & Shabbat ⍥

The Talmud (Shab. 30a/b) tells a wonderful story of King David and Shabbat. King David was very curious to discover when he would die. Finally David asked G-d, "Please, let me know my end."

G-d responded, " It is a decree before Me that a person's end is not made known."

David, however, was persistent, "So tell me the measure of my days!" he said. Again G-d refused and said, "It is a decree before me that a person's span of life is not made known."

Again David persisted. "Then let me know how frail I am."

Finally G-d responded, "You will die on Shabbat."

David was unhappy with this and so he said, "Let me die on the first day of the week."

G-d refused.

Ever persistent, David said, "Then let me die Sabbath eve."

G-d responded, "Better to me is one day that you sit and learn than the thousands of burnt offerings which your son Solomon is destined to sacrifice before Me!"

So every Shabbat David spent hours occupied in learning.

Then, on the Shabbat when David was meant to die, the Angel of death stood before him but found it impossible to prevail against him because David did not cease learning and as we know from the Talmud (*Sotah* 21a), the Angel of death cannot approach someone who is studying the Torah.

So the Angel of death couldn't figure out what to do. He then spied a garden in front of David's house. The Angel of death ascended the ladder and made noise in the trees. David heard the noise and went out and climbed the ladder to look. The ladder broke underneath him and he died.

V'ZOT HATORAH
("This is the Torah")

A 444 B 191 BC 373 L 187 DP 251

Cong. recites aloud or sings in unison.
**V'zot hatorah asher sam Moshe,
lifnay b'nay Yisrael, al pee Adonai, b'yad Moshe.**
("This is the Torah that Moses placed before
the Children of Israel at the command of G-d.")

☙ READING FROM THE PROPHETS ❧

A section from the Prophets, having a connection to the Torah Portion, is chanted. This is known as the *Haftarah* reading.

☙ SPECIAL PRAYERS ❧

Before returning the Torah to the *Aron*, some synagogues insert special prayers on behalf of the government and for the welfare of the State of Israel. In some congregations, memorial prayers are also recited. When the Blessing of the New Month is not recited, the Torah is returned to the *Aron* (see page 62).

☙ BLESSING OF THE NEW MONTH ❧

If *Rosh Chodesh* (the new month) falls during the ensuing week, special prayers welcoming the new month are now recited.

In ancient days, The *Sanhedrin* (legislature) fixed the day(s) of the new month upon the earliest sighting of the new moon by witnesses. When the Jews were exiled, Hillel formed the calendar, and later it became the custom to publicly announce the coming of the new month on the Shabbat preceding the actual days. This was done simply because Shabbat was the time of the greatest gathering of Jews during the week. It is interesting to note that the prayer for the new month contains many supplications, eleven of which are preceded by the word *chayim* (life), where we ask G-d for a life of goodness and blessing, a life of long years.... The *Gaon* of Vilna stated that the recital of the word *chayim*, corresponds to the eleven times during the year (except in a leap year) that we bless the new month. The new month of *Tishray* is not blessed since the first day of that month is *Rosh Hashanah*, which takes preference over *Rosh Chodesh*.

The following is a short summary of the prayers for the Blessing of the New Month:

Y'hee Ratzon
("May it be Your will")

The actual prayer for *Rosh Chodesh* is recited by the Congregation and repeated by the *Chazan*.

Moled

An announcement by the Rabbi or Sexton of the exact moment that the appearance of the new moon will take place.

Mee Sheh-asah Neesim
("He Who performed miracles")

This prayer for our redemption is recited by the Congregation and repeated by the *Chazan*.

Announcement of the day(s) of Rosh Chodesh

The day(s) of *Rosh Chodesh* are recited by the *Chazan* and repeated aloud by the Congregation.

Y'chad-shay-hu
("May it [the new month] be renewed")

This short supplication is recited by the Congregation and repeated by the *Chazan*.

Y'HEE RATZON
("May it be Your will")

A 452 B 199 BC 381 DP 261

Y'hee ratzon milfanecha,
Adonai Elohaynu, vaylohay avotaynu,
Sheh-t'chadaysh alaynu
Et hachodesh hazeh l'tovah v'livrachah.
V'teetayn lanu Chayim aruchim,
Chayim shel shalom, Chayim shel tovah,
Chayim shel brachah, Chayim shel parnasah,

Chayim shel cheelutz atzamot,
Chayim sheh-yaysh ba-hem yirat shamayim v'yirat chayt,
Chayim sheh-ayn ba-hem bushah uch'leemah,
Chayim shel osher v'chavod.
Chayim sheh-t'hay vanu ahavat Torah v'yirat shamayim,
Chayim sheh-yi-malu mishalot leebaynu l'tovah, Amen, Selah.

The actual moment that *Rosh Chodesh* will take place, i.e., the re-appearance of the new moon (the *Moled*), is then announced.

MEE SHEH-ASAH NEESIM
("He Who has created miracles")

A 452 **B** 199 **BC** 381 **L** 191 **DP** 261

Congregation recites, Chazan *repeats.*

Mee sheh-asah neesim la-avotaynu,
v'ga-al otam may-avdut l'chayrut,
Hu yigal otanu b'karov,
vee-ka-baytz needachaynu may-arba kanfot ha-aretz,
chavayrim kal Yisrael, v'nomar Amen

The *Chazan* holds the Torah scroll on his right side and announces the day(s) that *Rosh Chodesh* will occur.

Chazan *recites aloud,* Cong. *repeats aloud.*

Rosh Chodesh...*(insert name of month)*

MarCheshvan (Oct./Nov.)	*Kislev* (Nov./Dec.)
Tevet (Dec./Jan.)	*Sh'vat* (Jan./Feb.)
Adar (Feb./Mar.)	*Nissan* (Mar./Apr.)
Iyar (Apr./May)	*Sivan* (May/June)

Tamuz (June/July) ☙ *Menachem Av* (July/Aug.) ☙ *Elul* (Aug./Sept.)

Yihyeh b'yom...*(insert day(s) of the week)*

HaRishon—Sunday	*HaR'vee-ee*—Wednesday
HaShaynee—Monday	*HaChamee-shee*—Thursday
HaShleeshee—Tuesday	*HaShee-shee*—Friday
HaShabbat—Shabbat	

(When Rosh Chodesh *falls on two days,*
insert the word **oov'yom** *[and on the day] followed by the next day.)*

ha-bah alaynu v'al kal Yisrael, l'tovah.

Y'CHAD-SHAYHU
("May it be renewed")

A 452 B 199 BC 381 L 191 DP 261

This is the concluding prayer of the Blessing of the New Month. We pray that G-d will bless the new month for us for life and peace, joy and gladness, salvation and consolation. When the *Chazan* repeats the prayer, the Congregation responds *Amen* after hearing each of the petitions.

Cong. recites, Chazan *repeats.*

Y'chad-shayhu Hakadosh Baruch Hu,
Alaynu v'al kal Yisrael,
L'chayim ul'shalom *Cong. responds* Amen.
L'sason ul'simchah *Cong. responds* Amen.
Lee-shu-ah ul'nechamah *Cong. responds* Amen.
v'nomar Amen *Cong. responds* Amen.

🕿 THE TORAH IS RETURNED TO THE ARON 🕿

A series of special prayers, concluding with the hope that Israel should be worthy of being host to G-d's holiness and asking that G-d renew the days of the old are said at this point.

Prior to these prayers, the Psalm of *Ashray* ("Fortunate") is recited.

The Torah scroll is lifted and escorted back to the Aron. *It is once again carried around to the Congregation and during the procession, the following hymns are chanted.*

Y'HAL'LU
("Let them Praise")

A 458 B 205 BC 387 L 193 DP 267

Chazan *recites:* **Y'hal'lu et shaym, Adonai,**
kee nisgav sh'mo l'vado.

Cong. responds: **Hodo al eretz v'shamayim,**
vayah-rem keren l'amo,
t'heelah l'chol chasseedav,
livnay Yisrael am k'rovo, Halleluyah.

MIZMOR L'DAVID

("A Psalm to David"—Psalm 29)

A 458 **BC** 387 **B** 205 **DP** 267

The Torah was given to the Jewish people at Mount Sinai on the Shabbat. Several allusions to the Shabbat are contained in this Psalm, including the mentioning of the word "*Kol*" (voice) seven times.

Chazan and Cong. recite or sing together.

**Mizmor L'David
Havu LaAdonai b'nay aylim,
havu LaAdonai kavod va-oz,
havu LaAdonai kavod sh'mo,
hishta-cha-vu LaAdonai
b'hadrat kodesh.**

**Kol Adonai al hamahyim,
El haka-vod hir-im
Adonai al mahyim rabim.**

**Kol Adonai ba-ko-ach,
kol Adonai b'hadar,
kol Adonai shovayr arazim,
vai-sha-bayr Adonai
et arzay halvanon.**

**Va-yarkidaym k'mo aygel,
l'vanon v'siryon k'mo ven r'aymim.**

**Kol Adonai chotzayv lahavot aysh,
kol Adonai yachil midbar,
yachil Adonai midbar kadaysh,
kol Adonai y'cholayl ayalot.**

**Va-ye-chesof y'arot,
uv'haychalo kulo omayr kavod.**

**Adonai lamabul yashav,
vayayshev Adonai melech l'olam.
Adonai oz l'amo yeetayn,
Adonai y'varaych et amo vashalom.**

ॐ *Amen* ॐ

ow often have you said the word *Amen*? A hundred times? A thousand times? In fact, the Sages carefully arranged the daily prayers in such a fashion that everyone would have the chance to respond to one hundred *Amens* each and every day. Yet its meaning remains a mystery to most of us.

A multitude of traditional Jewish sources testify to the great power contained in this small and simple word. The Talmud in Tractate *Sanhedrin*, for instance, states that the very gates of Heaven will open for one who answers *Amen* with all of one's strength. (In other words, G-d will heed one's prayers.) Other sources state that saying *Amen* has the power to annul a harsh Heavenly decree. Rabbi Yudan, in the *Midrash Rabbah*, states that whoever answers *Amen* in this world will merit the reward of answering *Amen* in the World-to-Come.

All of this power rests in one simple word. So what does *Amen* actually mean? *Amen*, in Hebrew, is made of the three letters—*Aleph*, *Mem* and *Nun* and is an acronym for *El Melech Neeman*, meaning, "G-d is a faithful King."

When we say *Amen*, we affirm our trust in G-d that He will fulfill the promises He has made. For this reason, the Talmud states that a child reaches the point of being worthy of a share in the World-to-Come only when he or she is old enough to answer *Amen*. From this point, the child has established his or her faith in G-d as a reality.

In connection with this, the *Sefer HaChasidim* states that by reciting one's blessings quietly, one commits a grave sin, for the people in hearing distance are prevented from hearing and responding *Amen*, and thus from meriting this long list of great rewards.

So the next time you say *Amen*, know the significance of this most powerful word and say it with meaning!

ETZ CHAYIM HEE
("It is a tree of life")

A 460 **BC** 389 **B** 207 **DP** 271

These are the concluding verses to the prayer *Uvenuchu Yomar* ("And when the *Aron* rested, he (Moses) would say"). This prayer expresses Moses' hope and our wish as well that the *Aron* of the Lord would find its resting place and that the days of old, when we had our Holy Temple, will once again be renewed. Often the Congregation and *Chazan* sing these verses together.

The Aron *is opened, the Torah is returned to its holy place and the following hymn is sung.*

**Etz chayim hee, lamachazeekim bah,
v'tomcheha m'ushar.
D'ra-che-ha, darchay no-am,
v'chal n'teevoteh-hah shalom.**

**Hasheevaynu Adonai,
Aylechah v'na-shu-vah,
chadaysh, yamaynu, k'kedem.**

After returning the Torah to the *Aron* and prior to the continuation of our prayers, a Torah thought, a sermon or discussion by the Rabbi may take place, usually related to the Torah Portion of the week or concerning current events of interest to Jews.

ॠ *The Pious Cow* ॠ

here is an old story of a Jewish man who owned a plowing cow. Six days a week the cow plowed the land, but just as the Jewish man rested on the Shabbat, so did the cow. In time, the pious man's wealth slipped away and he was forced to sell his cow to a gentile man. The faithful cow worked the land during the week, but on the Shabbat, she lay down under the yoke and would not work. Through repeated beatings, the cow would not budge from her place. Seeing this, the gentile man returned to the Jew, and said to him, "Take back your cow, for she works all the week, but when I take her out on the Shabbat, she refuses to move."

When the Jewish man heard this, he immediately understood that the cow had become accustomed to resting on the Shabbat and said to the gentile, "Come, I will get her up and make her plow." When he approached the cow, he whispered in her ear, "Alas, pious cow, when you were in my possession, you rested on the Shabbat, but now you must do the will of your new master." With that, the cow immediately arose to plow the fields.

The gentile man, astonished at the results, asked the Jewish man, "What did you whisper to her? You must tell me or I won't take leave of you!" The pious man related his actions. When the gentile heard this he was shaken as he drew an inference to himself. "If this creature which has no speech, no intelligence, no understanding, affirms her Creator, shall not I, whom the Holy One created in his own image and likeness, with understanding, wisdom and intelligence, shall I not affirm my Creator?" At once he became a righteous convert.

7

Mussaf
The Additional Service

ussaf is the additional service recited on every *Shabbat*, New Moon and Festival. The name *Mussaf* actually means "additional" and it commemorates, as well as replaces, the extra sacrifices that were offered on special days in our ancient Great Temple in Jerusalem. These additions to the daily Temple Service symbolized the added holiness of the *Shabbat* or Festival. Since we no longer have the Great Temple, we offer our prayers today in place of the Priestly Service and in place of the sacrifices.

The main part of the *Mussaf* Service consists of the *Shemoneh Esray* recited quietly by the Congregation and the *Chazan*'s repetition.

⅋ HALF KADDISH ⅋

Here, the Half *Kaddish* introduces the *Shemoneh Esray*. In this beautiful and ancient prayer we ask that G-d's name be exalted throughout the world. The most important part is the Congregational response, *Amen, Y'hay sh'may rabbah m'varach...* ("May His great name be blessed forever and ever"), which should be recited aloud and fervently.

Chazan *recites:* **Yitgadal, v'yitkadash, sh'may rabbah.**
Cong. responds Amen.

B'almah di-v'ra chirutay, v'yamlich malchutay, b'chayaychon uv'yomaychon, u'v'chayay d'chol bayt Yisrael, ba-agalah uvizman kareev, v'imru, Amen. *Cong. responds* Amen.

Chazan *and Cong. recite together:* **Y'hay sh'may rabbah m'varach, l'alam ul'almay almahyah.**

Chazan *recites:* **Yitbarach, v'yishtabach, v'yit-pa-ar, v'yit-romam, v'yit-naseh, v'yit-hadar, v'yit-aleh, v'yit-halal, sh'may d'kudshah, B'rich Hu.** *Cong. responds* B'rich Hu.

L'aylah, min kol birchatah v'shiratah, tushb'chatah, v'ne-chematah, da-amiran b'almah, v'imru, Amen.
Cong. responds Amen.

ॐ SHEMONEH ESRAY ℘
("Silent Devotion")

A 462 **B** 209 **BC** 391 **L** 193 **DP** 277

The *Shemoneh Esray* or *Amidah* is the highlight of the *Mussaf* Service, and like all the daily silent devotional prayers it is divided into three sections.

Praise—In the first three blessings of the Silent Devotion, we recognize, describe and praise the glory of G-d.

Petition—The middle blessing expresses the sanctity of the day. This blessing also asks G-d to restore the Holy Temple Service.

Thanksgiving—The final three blessings express our gratitude to G-d and include a prayer for peace as well as a personal prayer asking G-d to protect us.

On the Shabbat of *Rosh Chodesh* the middle section (Petition) contains special supplemental prayers and is substituted in place of the regular section.

Since the *Mussaf Amidah* is the most important *Shemoneh Esray* of the day, it should be recited with particular concentration and devotion. We have included no transliteration since the *Shemoneh Esray* is recited quietly. *For further explanation of*

Shemoneh Esray, *see pages 17-19 and 44-45.*

℘ CHAZARAT HASHATZ ℵ
("*Chazan*'s Repetition")

A 462 **B** 209 **BC** 391 **L** 193 **DP** 277

In a Congregational setting, when one prays with a *minyan*, the *Shemoneh Esray* is repeated aloud by the *Chazan*. Included in the repetition is the recital of the *Kedushah* which is the most important part of the *Chazan*'s repetition.

℘ KEDUSHAH ℵ
("Sanctification of G-d's Name")

A 464 **B** 211 **BC** 393 **L** 193 **DP** 279

The *Kedushah* is probably the holiest prayer of the service. It offers an opportunity to publicly declare and affirm G-d's holiness. Written by the men of the Great Assembly in the early part of the Second Temple period, the most important verses are *Kadosh, Kadosh, Kadosh* (Holy, Holy, Holy), *Baruch K'vod* (Blessed is the Glory) and *Yimloch* (May G-d Reign). The first verse, *Na-areetz'cha* (we will reverse) is an introduction to the *Kedushah*.

During the *Kedushah* it is customary to stand and keep one's feet together and then slightly rise three times on one's toes at the recital of the words *Kadosh, Kadosh, Kadosh*. Then we rise again once on our toes at the recital of the words *Baruch K'vod Adonai* and *Yimloch Adonai*. In this way we rise as the angels rose toward Heaven, as we find in Isaiah 6:2: "Above him stood the angels and with two [wings they] did fly."

Cong. recites, Chazan *repeats.*

Na-areetz'cha v'nakdeesh'cha,
K'sod see-ach sarfay kodesh,
Hamakdeeshim shimcha bakodesh,
Ka-katuv al yad n'vee-echa,
V'karah zeh el zeh, v'amar.

Cong. and Chazan *together. During the first three words we rise on our toes.*
Kadosh, Kadosh, Kadosh, Adonai Tz'va-ot,

Meloh Chol Ha-aretz K'vodo.

Cong. recites, Chazan *repeats. During the word* K'vodo *we rise on our toes.*

**K'vodo maleh olam, m'shartav sho-alim zeh lazeh,
ayeh m'kom k'vodo, l'umatam baruch yomayru.**

Cong. and Chazan *together. During the word* Baruch *we rise on our toes.*

Baruch K'vod Adonai Mimkomo.

Cong. recites, Chazan *repeats.*

**Mimkomo hu yifen b'rachamim,
v'yachon am ham'yachadim sh'mo,
erev vavoker, b'chol yom tamid,
pa-amayim b'ahavah shema omrim.**

Cong. recites, Chazan *repeats.*

**Shema Yisrael, Adonai Eloheinu, Adonai Echad.
Hu Elohaynu, Hu Aveenu, Hu Malkaynu, Hu Mo-shee-aynu.
V'hu yashmee-aynu b'rachamav shayneet l'aynay kol chai.
Lihyot lachem lay-lohim.
Ani Adonai Elohaychem.**

Cong. recites, Chazan *repeats.*

Uv'divray kad-sh'cha katuv laymor.

Cong. and Chazan *together. During the word* Yimloch *we rise on our toes.*

**Yimloch Adonai L'olam, Elohayich Tziyon,
L'dor Vador, Halleluyah.**

The *Chazan* continues with the repetition of the *Shemoneh Esray.* In many synagogues, the *Chazan* and the congregation will sing together the following paragraphs during the repetition.

UV'YOM HASHABBAT
("And on the Shabbat day")

A 468 B 215 BC 395 L 195 DP 285

This paragraph from Numbers (28:9-10) describes the additional offerings and sacrifices of the Shabbat in the days of the Temple.

**Uv'yom haShabbat, sh'nay ch'vasim
b'nay shanah t'mimim.**

Ush'nay esronim solet,
mincha b'lulah vashemen v'niskoh.
Olat Shabbat b'shabbato, al olat h'atamid v'niskah.

YISM'CHU V'MALCHUTCHA
("They will rejoice in Your kingship")

A 468 **B** 217 **BC** 395 **L** 195 **DP** 285

Those who observe and sanctify the Shabbat will rejoice in
G-d's kingship. G-d called the Seventh day—the Shabbat—"a
remembrance of Creation."

**Yism'chu v'malchut'cha
shomray Shabbat v'kor-ay oneg,
am m'kad'shay sh'vee-ee,
kulam yisb'u v'yitangu meetu-vecha,
uva-sh'vee-ee, ratzeeta bo v'keedashto,
chemdat yamim oto karata,
zaycher l'ma-asay v'raysheet.**

ELOHAYNU
("Our G-d")

A 468 **B** 217 **BC** 395 **L** 196 **DP** 287

We ask G-d to be pleased with our rest and to help us serve
Him sincerely. We end with a blessing "Blessed are You, oh G-d,
who sanctifies the Shabbat."

**Elohaynu, vaylohay avotaynu,
r'tzay vim'nuchataynu,
kad'shaynu b'mitzvotecha,
v'tayn chel-kaynu b'toratecha,
sab-aynu mee-tuvecha,
v'samchaynu beey'shu-atecha,
v'ta-hayr leebaynu l'avd'cha b'emet.
V'hanchee-laynu Adonai Elohaynu,
b'ahavah uv'ratzon Shabbat kadshecha,
v'yanuchu vo Yisrael m'kadshay sh'mechah.
Baruch ata Adonai, m'kadaysh haShabbat.**

THE *CHAZAN'S* REPETITION CONTINUES.
AT THE *MODIM* PRAYER WE RISE AND BOW AT THE
WORD *MODIM* AS THE *CHAZAN* RECITES *MODIM* ALOUD.

SIM SHALOM
("Establish peace")

A 472 **B** 221 **BC** 403 **L** 198 **DP** 291

We end the *Chazan's* repetition with this prayer of peace, asking G-d to establish peace, compassion and goodness upon all Jews.

Sim shalom tovah uv'racha,
chayn, va-chesed, v'rachamim,
alaynu v'al kol Yisrael amecha.
Barchaynu aveenu, kulanu k'echad b'or panecha,
ki v'or panecha nata-ta lanu Adonai Elohaynu,
torat chayim, v'ahavat chesed,
utz'dakah, uv'racha, v'rachamim, v'chayim, v'shalom.
V'tov b'ay-necha l'varaych et amcha Yisrael,
b'chol ayt, uv'chol sha-ah, bishlomechah.
Baruch ata Adonai, ham'va-raych et amo Yisrael bashalom.

☜ KADDISH SHALAYM ☞
("Full *Kaddish*")

A 474 **B** 223 **BC** 405 **L** 74 **DP** 325

The *Chazan* now recites the *Kaddish Shalaym* which is the concluding part of the *Shemoneh Esray*. We pray that our service will be accepted. The Congregation recites the appropriate responses aloud, with concentration and devotion, especially *Amen* and the words *Y'hay Sh'may Rabbah M'varach...* ("May His great name be blessed forever and ever").

Chazan *recites:*
Yitgadal, v'yitkadash, sh'may rabbah. *Cong. responds* Amen.

B'almah di-v'ra chirutay, v'yamlich malchutay,
b'chayaychon uv'yomaychon, u'v'chayay d'chol

bayt Yisrael, ba-agalah uvizman kareev,
v'imru, Amen. *Cong. responds* Amen.

Chazan *and Cong. recite together:* **Y'hay sh'may rabbah
m'varach, l'alam ul'almay almahyah.**

Chazan *recites:*

**Yitbarach, v'yishtabach, v'yit-pa-ar, v'yit-romam,
v'yit-naseh, v'yit-hadar, v'yit-aleh, v'yit-halal,
sh'may d'kudshah, B'rich Hu.** *Cong. responds* B'rich Hu.

**L'aylah, min kol birchatah v'shiratah,
tush-b'chatah, v'ne-chematah, da-amiran b'almah,
v'imru, Amen.** *Cong. responds* Amen.

**Titkabel tz'lot-hon u-va-ut-hon d'chol
bayt Yisrael, kadam avu-hon di vish-maya,
v'imru, Amen.** *Cong. responds* Amen.

**Y'hay sh'lama rabbah min sh'maya, v'chayim,
alaynu v'al kol Yisrael, v'imru, Amen.** *Cong. responds* Amen.

**Oseh shalom bimro-mav, Hu ya-aseh shalom,
alaynu v'al kol Yisrael, v'imru, Amen.** *Cong. responds* Amen.

☜ CONCLUDING HYMNS ☞

At the conclusion of the Prayer Services we express our joy through song. This reflects our confidence in G-d that He has accepted our prayers. We will sing the following songs:

1. *Ayn Kaylohaynu*—Song of Devotion
2. *Alaynu*—Declaration of Faith
3. *Anim Zemirot*—Hymn of Glory
4. *Mizmor Shir*—Psalm of the Day
5. *Adon Olam*—Concluding Hymn

AYN KAYLOHAYNU
("There is none like our G-d")

A 476 B 225 BC 407 L 198 DP 327

This hymn of praise declares five aspects attributed to our G-d.
1. There is none like our G-d, 2. [There is no one] who is like our

G-d, 3. Let us thank our G-d, 4. Blessed is our G-d and finally, 5. You are our G-d. The Hebrew initials of the first three aspects (*Ayn*, *Mi*, *Nodeh*) spell out the word *Amen*.

Cong. and Chazan *sing together:*

Ayn Kaylohaynu,   Ayn KaAdonaynu,
Ayn K'malkaynu,   Ayn K'moshee-aynu.

Mee Chaylohaynu,   Mee ChaAdonaynu,
Mee Ch'malkaynu,   Mee Ch'moshee-aynu.

Nodeh Laylohaynu,   Nodeh LaAdonaynu,
Nodeh L'malkaynu, Nodeh L'moshee-aaynu.

Baruch Elohaynu,   Baruch Adonaynu,
Baruch Malkaynu,   Baruch Moshee-aynu.

Ata hu Elohaynu,   Ata hu Adonaynu,
Ata hu Malkaynu,   Ata hu Moshee-aynu.

Ata hu sheh-hikteeru, avotaynu,
L'fanecha, et ketoret hasamim.

ALAYNU

("It is our duty")

A 480 B 231 **BC** 413 **L** 200 **DP** 333

For more than 700 years this has been the final prayer of each of the daily prayers, as well as Festival and Sabbath prayers. In the 9th century, Rabbi Hai Ben David Gaon wrote that this sublime prayer was composed by Joshua as he brought the children of Israel into the promised land. Similar to the *Shema*, it declares our faith and expresses our gratitude for being able to serve G-d. Throughout the centuries, *Alaynu* was prohibited or censored in many countries. In particular the line in *Alaynu* stating "they [the other nations] bow to vanity and emptiness..." was considered an attack on other religions and was censored in Europe. In fact, it is still omitted from many prayer books.

Alaynu l'shabayach la-adon hakol,
latayt g'dula l'yotzayr b'raysheet.
Shelo asanu k'goyay ha-aratzot,

v'lo samanu k'mishp'chot ha-adama.
Sheh-lo sam chelkaynu kahem,
v'goralaynu k'chol hamonam.

(Chazan and Congregation bow at the underlined words)
Va-anachnu <u>kor'im</u> <u>umishtachavim</u> umodim,
lifnay melech malchay ham'lachim,
Hakadosh Baruch Hu.

Shehu noteh shamayim v'yosed aretz,
umoshav y'karo bashamayim meema-al,
oosh'cheenat oozo b'govhay m'romim.
Hu Elohaynu, ayn od.
Emet malkaynu, efes zulato,
ka-katuv b'torato, v'yadata hayom va-hashay-vota
el l'vavecha, kee Adonai hu ha-Elohim
bashamayim meema-al, v'al ha-aretz meetachat ayn od.

The final verse:
V'ne-emar, v'haya Adonai l'melech al kol ha-aretz,
bayom ha-hu yihyeh Adonai echad ush'mo echad.

ॐ KADDISH YATOM ॐ
("Mourner's *Kaddish*")

A 482 B 231 BC 413 DP 337

The Mourner's *Kaddish* is recited at every Congregational Service for eleven months following the death of a parent. It is also recited on the yearly anniversary (*Yahrtzeit*) of the parent's death. *Kaddish* is a source of merit for the soul and the most important part is the Congregational response, "*Amen, Y'hay shmay rabbah m'varach....*"

Mourner recites:
Yitgadal, v'yitkadash, sh'may rabbah.
B'almah di-v'ra chirutay, v'yamlich malchutay,
b'chayaychon uv'yomaychon, uv'chayay d'chol
bayt Yisrael, ba-agalah uvizman kareev, v'imru, Amen.

Cong. responds Amen.

Mourner and Cong. recite together: **Y'hay shmay rabbah m'varach,**
l'alam ul'almay almahya.

Mourner recites:

**Yitbarach, v'yishtabach, v'yitpa-ar, v'yitromam,
v'yitnaseh, v'yit-ha-dar, v'yit-aleh, v'yit-halal,
sh'may d'kudshah, B'rich Hu.** *Cong. responds* B'rich Hu.

**L'aylah, min kol birchatah v'shiratah,
tushb'chatah, v'ne-chematah,
da-amiran b'almah, v'imru, Amen.** *Cong. responds* Amen.

**Y'hay shlamah rabbah min sh'mayah, v'chayim,
alaynu v'al kol Yisrael, v'imru, Amen.** *Cong. responds* Amen.

**Oseh shalom bimromav, hu ya-aseh shalom,
alaynu v'al kol Yisrael, v'imru, Amen.** *Cong. responds* Amen.

ANIM ZEMIROT
("Hymn of Glory")

A 484 B 233 BC 415 DP 339

This beautiful hymn is recited responsively. It is an alphabetical arrangement depicting G-d's glory.

The *Aron* is opened and the *Chazan* recites the first verse, the Congregation says the second verse and each verse is alternately recited in the same manner.

Chazan *recites:* **Anim zemirot v'shirim eh-eh-rog,
kee aylecha nafshi ta-arog.**

Chazan *and Cong. recite together:*
Nafshee chomdah b'tzayl yadecha, lada-at kol roz sodecha.

Chazan *recites:*
Meeday dabree bichvodecha, homeh leebee el dodecha.

Chazan *and Cong. recite together:*
**Al kayn adaber b'chah nichbadot,
v'shimcha achabayd b'sheeray y'deedot.**

Chazan *recites:*
**Asaprah ch'vodcha v'lo r'eeteecha, adamcha,
achancha v'lo yedaateecha.**

Chazan *and Cong. recite together:*
**B'yad n'vee-echa b'sod avadecha,
deemeeta hadar k'vod hodecha.**

Chazan *recites:*
G'dulatcha ug'vuratecha, keenu l'tokef p'ulatecha.

Chazan *and Cong. recite together:*
Deemu otcha v'lo k'fee yeshcha,
vayashvucha l'fee ma-asecha.

Chazan *recites:*
Himsheelucha b'rov chezyonot,
hincha echad b'chol dimyonot.

Chazan *and Cong. recite together:*
Vayechezu v'cha ziknah uvacharut,
us'ar rosh-cha b'sayvah v'shacharut.

Chazan *recites:*
Ziknah b'yom din, uvacharut b'yom k'rav,
k'eesh milchamot yadav lo rav.

Chazan *and Cong. recite together:*
Chavash kovah y'shuah b'rosho,
hoshee-ah lo y'meeno uz'roah kadsho.

Chazan *recites:*
Tal'lay orot rosho nimla, k'vutzotav r'seesay lailah.

Chazan *and Cong. recite together:*
Yitpa-er bee kee chafetz bee, v'hu yihyeh lee la-ateret tz'vee.

Chazan *recites:*
Ketem tahor paz, d'mut rosho,
v'chak al maytzach k'vod shem kadsho.

Chazan *and Cong. recite together:*
L'chayn ul'chavod tz'vee tifarah, umato lo itra atara.

Chazan *recites:*
Machl'fot rosho k'veemay v'churot,
k'vutzotav taltalim sh'chorot.

Chazan *and Cong. recite together:*
N'vay hatzedek tz'vee tifarto, ya-aleh na al rosh simchato.

Chazan *recites:*
S'gulato t'hee na v'yado ateret,
utz'neef m'luchah tz'vee tiferet.

Chazan *and Cong. recite together:*
Amusim n'sa-am ateret indam,

may-asher yakru v'aynav kibdam.

Chazan *recites:*
P'ayro alai uf'ayree alav, v'karov aylai b'karee ailav.

Chazan *and Cong. recite together:*
Tzach v'adom lil'vusho adom,
purah b'dorcho b'vo-oh mayedom.

Chazan *recites:*
Kesher t'fillin her-ah le-anav,
t'munat Adonai l'neged aynav.

Chazan *and Cong. recite together:*
Rotzeh v'amo anavim y'fa-ayr,
yoshayv t'heelot bam l'hitpa-er.

Chazan *recites:*
Rosh d'varcha emet koray mayrosh,
dor vador am doreshcha d'rosh.

Chazan *and Cong. recite together:*
Sheet hamon sheerai na alecha,
v'reenati tikrav aylechah.

Chazan *recites:*
T'heelatee t'hee na l'roshcha ateret,
ut'feelati teekon k'toret.

Chazan *and Cong. recite together:*
Teekar sheerat rash b'aynecha,
kahshir yushar al korbanecha.

Chazan *recites:*
Birchatee ta-aleh l'rosh mashbeer,
m'cholayl umo-leed tzadeek kabeer.

Chazan *and Cong. recite together:*
Uvirchatee t'na-anah lee rosh,
v'otah kach l'chah kivsamim rosh.

Chazan *and Cong. recite together:*
Ye-erav na seechee alecha, kee nafshee ta-arog aylecha.

PSALM OF THE DAY

The Psalm of the day, which for Shabbat is Psalm 92 is recited
and is followed by the Mourner's *Kaddish* (see page 23).

ADON OLAM
("Eternal Lord")

A 12 B 77 BC 423 DP 359

This hymn expresses our absolute trust in G-d's omnipotence and permanence. While *Olam* can mean both eternity and world, here it is generally understood to refer to the eternity of the Lord.

Adon Olam has been attributed to various medieval poets, and was most likely written by the Spanish poet Solomon Ibn Gabriol in the 11th century, although it may date back to Babylonian times.

**Adon olam asher malach, b'terem kol y'tzir nivrah,
L'ayt na-a-sa b'cheftzo kol, ahzay melech sh'mo nikrah.**

**V'acharay kichlot ha-kol, l'vado yimloch norah,
V'hu haya v'hu hoveh, v'hu yihyeh b'tifarah.**

**V'hu echad, v'ayn shaynee, l'hamsheel lo l'hachbirah,
B'li raysheet, b'li tachlit, v'lo ha-ohz v'hamisrah.**

**V'hu ayli, v'chai go-ali, v'tzur chevli b'ayt tzarah,
V'hu neesee u-manos lee, m'nat kosee b'yom ekrah.**

**B'yado afkid ruchee, b'ayt eeshan v'ah-eerah,
V'im ruchee g'veeyatee, Adonai lee v'lo eerah.**

SHABBAT SHALOM — GOOD SHABBOS

One leaves the synagogue content and filled with confidence that our prayers will be accepted. We greet each other with *Shabbat Shalom*, or *Good Shabbos*. In some synagogues *Kiddush* is recited and cake, fish, and in some cases, *kugels* are served. Otherwise, we go home, recite the *Kiddush* and enjoy a festive meal complete with Shabbat *Zemirot*.

It is ideal to spend the balance of the day reading from Psalms, relaxing, or studying other books and meditating on this holy day of rest.

℀ SHABBAT MORNING KIDDUSH ℞

A 492 B 249 BC 423 L 202 DP 611

The *Shabbat* Morning *Kiddush* was instituted by the Rabbis in honor of *Shabbat*. It is customary to recite various Biblical verses,

prior to the actual blessing. We have included two paragraphs from
Exodus that were added to the *Kiddush* over the centuries attesting
to the commandments to keep *Shabbat*.

**V'shamru v'nay Yisrael et haShabbat, la-asot et
haShabbat l'dorotam brit olam. Baynee oovayn
B'nay Yisrael, ot hee l'olam, kee shayshet yamim
asah Adonai et hasha-mayim v'et ha'aretz,
oovayom hash'vee-ee shavat va-yee-nafash.** (Exod. 31:16-17)

**Zachor et yom haShabbat l'kadsho.
Shayshet yamim ta-avod,
v'asee-ta kal m'lachtecha,
v'yom hash'vee-ee Shabbat laAdonai Elohecha,
lo ta-aseh kal m'lacha, atah, oovincha, ooveetecha,
avd'cha, va-amat'cha, oov'hemtecha,
v'gayrcha asher bisharecha.
Kee shayshet yamim asah Adonai
et Hashamayim v'et ha-aretz,
et hayam vet kal asher bam,
vayanch bayom hash'vee'ee...**

**Al kayn bayrach Adonai,
et yom haShabbat, vay'kadshayhu.** (Exod. 20:8-11)

Savree maranan v'rabbanan v'robotai:
(Recite this blessing over wine or grape juice.)

**Baruch atah Adonai, Elohaynu melech ha-olam
boray p'ree hagafen.** *Listeners respond* Amen.

(Recite this blessing if you are using whiskey or another drink.)

**Baruch atah Adonai, Elohaynu melech ha-olam
sheh-hakol nih-yeh bidvaro.***Listeners respond* Amen.

Mincha
The Afternoon Service

℣ MINCHA ℟
("Afternoon Service")

A 502 **B** 251 **BC** 437 **L** 203 **DP** 363

incha is introduced by the prayers *Ashray* and *Uvah L'tziyon,* which are recited by the Congregation and the *Chazan* in unison.

℣ TORAH READING ℟
(Public Reading from the Torah)

A 508 **B** 257 **BC** 443 **L** 204 **DP** 371

Half *Kaddish* is recited and the first portion of the following week's Bible *Parsha* is publicly read.

The introductory hymns for the removal of the Torah from the *Aron* are recited.

Vay'hee Binsoah	(see page 55)
Beh Ana Rachitz	(see page 55)
Gadlu	(see page 56)
L'cha Adonai	(see page 56)

Three men, a *Kohayn*, a *Levi*, and a *Yisrael*, are called to recite blessings. *(Please refer to The Torah Reading Service, page 57, for transliteration.)*

After the reading, the Torah is lifted and the Congregation chants *V'zot Hatorah. (See page 59 for transliteration.)* The Torah Scroll is then returned to the *Aron* and the following hymns are recited.

Y'hal'lu	(see page 62)
L'David Mizmor	(Psalm 24)
Etz Chaim Hee	(see page 65)

In some congregations, memorial prayers are recited for those individuals who will observe *Yahrzeit* (anniversary of a death).

✺ HALF KADDISH ✺

A 514   B 263   BC 449   L 68   DP 379

The Half *Kaddish*, one of four different types of *Kaddish*, is the bridge that connects the various parts of the Service together. Here the Half *Kaddish* joins the section of the Torah Reading to the *Shemoneh Esray*. The most important part is the Congregational response, *Amen, Y'hay sh'may rabbah m'varach...*("May His great name be blessed forever and ever"), which should be fervently recited aloud. *(Please see page 16 for transliteration.)*

✺ SHEMONEH ESRAY ✺
("Silent Devotion")

A 514   B 263   BC 449   L 206   DP 381

The *Shemoneh Esray*, or *Amidah*, is exactly the same as the Evening Service. The *Amidah* should be recited softly. Many people gently rock during prayer as an aid to concentration. *(Please refer to pages 17-19 and 44-45 for an in-depth explanation.)*

✺ CHAZARAT HASHATZ ✺
("*Chazan*'s Repetition")

A 514   B 263   BC 449   L 206   DP 381

As in all the other services, the *Chazan*'s repetition is a communal prayer, and several of the most important parts of the service are included in the repetition. At various points, the *Aron* is opened and the Congregation rises. The highlight of the repetition is the *Kedushah*.

☙ KEDUSHAH ☙
("Sanctification of G-d's Name")

A 516 B 265 BC 451 L 206 DP 383

This is the most important part of the *Chazan*'s repetition. The *Kedushah* of *Mincha* is a modified version of the *Shacharit Kedushah*. It is customary to lift oneself on one's toes three times at the recital of *Kadosh, Kadosh, Kadosh...* and one time at the recital of *Baruch K'vod Adonai...* and *Yimloch Adonai*.

The Children of Israel join with the angels in praising G-d in the *Kedushah*.

Cong. and Chazan *together.*

**N'kadaysh et shimchah ba-olam,
k'shaym sheh-makdeeshim oto,
bishmay marom,
kakatuv al yad n'vee-echa,
v'karah zeh el zeh v'amar.**

Cong. and Chazan *together.*
During the words Kadosh, Kadosh, Kadosh, *we rise on our toes.*

**Kadosh, Kadosh, Kadosh,
Adonai Tz'va-ot, Meloh Chal Ha-aretz K'vodo.**

Chazan *recites.*

L'umatam baruch yomayru.

Cong. and Chazan *together. During the word* Baruch *we rise on our toes.*
Baruch K'vod Adonai Mimkomo.

Chazan *recites.*

Uv'divray kad-sh'cha katuv laymor.

Cong. and Chazan *together. During the word* Yimloch *we rise on our toes.*
**Yimloch Adonai L'olam, Elohayich Tziyon,
L'dor Vador, Halleluyah.**

⁊ KADDISH SHALAYM ℞
("Full *Kaddish*")

A 524 **B** 275 **BC** 461 **L** 74 **DP** 403

At the end of every Service, the *Chazan* recites the Reader's *Kaddish*, where G-d's name is magnified and sanctified and we trust that our prayers will be accepted. The Congregation should recite the appropriate responses with great concentration, especially *Amen, Y'hay sh'may rabbah m'varach.... (Please see the Evening Service page 21 for transliteration.)*

ALAYNU
("It is our duty")

A 526 **B** 275 **BC** 461 **L** 209 **DP** 405

For the last 700 years this has been the final prayer of each of the daily prayers, as well as each of the Festival and *Shabbat* prayers. In the 9th century Rabbi Hai Ben David Gaon wrote that this sublime prayer was composed by Joshua as he brought the Jews into the promised land. Throughout the centuries, *Alaynu* was prohibited or censored in many countries.

In the final prayer of the *Mincha Service* we place our belief and hope in G-d that He will re-affirm His Kingship amongst the nations of the world. *(Please see the Evening Service page 22 for transliteration.)*

If there are mourners in the synagogue, the Kaddish Yatom, *the Mourner's* Kaddish, *would follow* Alaynu. *(Please see the Evening Service page 23 for transliteration.)*

☜ *On Holy Soil* ☞

In the book *All For The Boss* by Ruchoma Shain we find this inspiring story.

Rabbi Yaakov Yosef Herman and his wife emigrated to Israel in mid-August 1939. They were scheduled to dock at Haifa port on a Wednesday; because of the impending war the boat docked on Friday, one hour before sunset. A few hours before that, World War II had erupted with the German invasion of Poland.

Loudspeakers ordered the passengers to disembark immediately. All the baggage from the hold of the ship would be unloaded onto the pier, and the passengers would have to remove it as quickly as possible.

Rabbi Herman and his wife were terribly upset. It would soon be Shabbat. How could they take care of their baggage when they had to immediately leave the port in order to get to Rabbi Alfa's house in Haifa in time for Shabbat?

Rabbi Herman grabbed the valise that contained his *Sefer Torah* and his *tallis* and *tefillin*, and Mrs. Herman took only her pocket-book. They edged their way through the pier and asked to be shown to the head customs officer.

A tall English officer listened as Rabbi Herman explained to him. "I have never desecrated the Shabbat in my life. To arrive in the Holy Land and desecrate it here is impossible," he said as tears rolled down his cheeks.

The officer answered curtly, "Rabbi this is *war*; you must make allowances."

"Just stamp our passports and let us through. We shall pick up our baggage after the Shabbat," Rabbi Herman pleaded.

"That's impossible. We are removing all the baggage from the ship and leaving it on the pier. Once the boat clears port, everything must be cleared off it also."

"I don't care about our baggage. Just stamp our passports so we can leave."

The officer looked at Rabbi Herman quizzically, "How much baggage have you?"

"Sixteen crates in the hold and nine suitcases in our cabin."

"Do you realize that once you leave here, your baggage will be on the pier with no one responsible for it? By tomorrow night you will not find a shred of your belongings. The Arabs will have stolen them all," the officer said emphatically.

"I have no alternative." replied Rabbi Herman. "It's almost time for the Shabbat. We must get to the city in time. Please, please, just clear our passports and let us go."

The officer, incredulous, called another English officer, "Stamp their passports and let them through. This rabbi is willing to lose all his belongings in order to get into the city in time for their Shabbat." The second officer stared at Rabbi Herman in amazement, as he stamped their passports and cleared their papers.

Rabbi and Mrs. Herman quickly grabbed a taxi and arrived at Rabbi Alfa's house just in time to light the candles.

That entire Shabbat, Rabbi Herman was spiritually elated. Over and over again he repeated, "The Boss does everything for me. What could I ever do for Him? Now at least I have the *zechus* (merit) to give all for the Boss for His *mitzvah* of Shabbat and to be *mekadesh Hashem* (sanctify G-d)."

Saturday night, after Rabbi Herman had waited the seventy-two minutes after sunset to *daven Maariv* and then make *Havdalah*, Rabbi Alfa suggested to him, "Let us go to the port. Maybe some of your crates are still there."

It was pitch dark at the port. However, they spied a little light at the far end. As they neared the lighted area, a clipped English voice rang out, "Who goes there?"

Rabbi Herman called out, "Some passengers from the boat that docked late yesterday afternoon."

The English guard approached them. "What's your name?" he asked tersely.

"Jacob J. Herman," he answered.

"Well, well, Rabbi it's about time you put in your appearance. I was assured that you would be here the minute the sun set. You are a few hours late! I have been responsible for your baggage for more than twenty-four hours. My commanding officer said he would have my head if any of your baggage was lost. Kindly check to see that all is in order and sign these papers. Please remove it all as quickly as possible...I am totally exhausted."

Maariv
The Concluding Service

❧ MAARIV ❧
(Concluding Service)

A 594 B 279 BC 535 L 106 DP 417

The *Shabbat* ends with the recital of the weekday Evening Service and the *Havdalah*.

❧ HAVDALAH ❧
("Separation")

A 618 B 551 L 234 DP 453

Heenay El y'shu-atee evtach, v'lo efchad,
kee azee v'zimrat yah, Adonai, vay'hee lee leey'shu-ah.
Ush'avtem mayim b'sason, mee-mai-nay hay'shu-ah.
LaAdonai hay'shu-ah, al amcha virchatecha selah,
Adonai tz'va-ot eemanu misgav lanu
Elohay Yaakov selah,

Adonai tz'va-ot ashray odom botayach boch,
Adonai hoshee-ah, hamelech ya-anaynu v'yom koraynu.
Lay'hudim hayta orah, v'simcha, v'sason, veekar.
Kayn tih-yeh lanu. kos y'shu-ot esah,
uv'shaym Adonai ekrah.

Blessing over the wine.
Baruch atah Adonai, Elohaynu melech ha-olam,
boray p'ree hagafen. *Listeners respond* Amen.

Blessing over the spices.
Baruch atah Adonai, Elohaynu melech ha-olam,
boray meenay v'samim. *Listeners respond* Amen.

After the blessing, smell the spices.

Blessing over the flame.
Baruch atah Adonai, Elohaynu melech ha-olam,
boray m'oray ha-aysh. *Listeners respond* Amen.

After the blessing, hold fingers near flame, see reflected light on fingernails.

Baruch atah Adonai, Elohaynu melech ha-olam,
hamavdeel bayn kodesh l'chol, bayn ohr l'cho-shech,
bayn yisrael la-amim, bayn yom hash'vee-ee
l'shayshet y'may hama-aseh.
Baruch atah Adonai, hamvdeel bayn kodesh l'chol.

Listeners respond Amen.

Zemirot
Shabbat Songs & Hymns

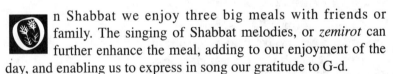

n Shabbat we enjoy three big meals with friends or family. The singing of Shabbat melodies, or *zemirot* can further enhance the meal, adding to our enjoyment of the day, and enabling us to express in song our gratitude to G-d.

Zemirot are not only exquisite Hebrew poems, but are fervent expressions of hope, thankfulness and prayer. Many were written by ancient Sages and Kabbalists and contain insights into creation. Others speak of our dedication to G-d and describe how we long to be close to Him. Still others movingly outline our love for Shabbat and invite everyone to join in thanking G-d for Shabbat and for our food. There are many *zemirot* in the *Siddur*. Some are universally popular while others are obscure. Some families sing several *zemirot* both during and after the meal, while other families may recite only one or two *zemirot*. Each family has different customs. When you share your Shabbat meal with others, you'll find that each family has favorite melodies. Learn from them all and soon you'll establish a repertoire of your own favorites!

ॐ ZEMIROT ॐ
("Shabbat Songs")

| A 362 | B 71 | BC 291 | DP 701 |

M'NUCHAH V'SIMCHAH
("Rest and Happiness")

| A 362 | BC 293 | DP 703 |

M'nuchah v'simchah ohr laihudim,
Yom Shabbaton yom machmadim,
Shomrov v'zochrav haymah m'eedim,
Kee l'sheeshah kol b'ru-im v'omdim.

Sh'may shamayim eretz v'yamim,
Kol tz'vah marom g'vohim v'ramim,
Tanin v'adam v'chayat r'aymim,
Kee b'yah Adonai tzur olamim.

Hu asher deebayr l'am s'gulato,
Shamor l'kadsho meebo-o v'ad tzayto,
Shabbat kodesh yom chemdato,
Kee voh shavat Ayl meekol m'lachto.

Bimitzvat Shabbat Ayl yachleetzach,
Kum k'rah aylov yochish l'amtzach,
Nishmat kol chai v'gam na-areetzach,
Echol b'simchah kee ch'var ratzach.

B'mishneh lechem v'keedush rabah,
B'rov matamim v'ru-ach n'deevah,
Yizku l'rav tuv hamitangim bah,
B'veeyat go-ayl l'cha-yay ha-olam habah.

Rest and happiness—light to the Jews, it is Shabbat, a day we protect and hold dear. Those who observe it testify that in six days all was created [including...] the heavens, the land and the sea, all forces of high, and all the high places, fish, humans and the animals; for G-d is the support for the entire universe. About Shabbat G-d spoke to His treasured nation, "Guard its sanctity from its beginning to its end." G-d holds the holy Shabbat dear, for on it He rested from His work. Through the mitzvah of Shabbat G-d will redeem you. Arise! Call to Him! He will strengthen you. (We recite,) "All the living," and also, "We proclaim Your strength." Eat with joy, for He has favored you. With double bread and special kiddush; with good food and a generous spirit. May those who enjoy Shabbat merit all that is good, with the coming of the Redeemer and the World to Come.

YAH RIBON

("G-d, the Master")

A 364 **B** 71 **BC** 295 **DP** 707

Yah ribon olam v'olmayah,
Ahnt hu malkah Melech malchayah.
Ovad givurtaych vitimhayah,
Sh'far kadamach l'hachavayah.

Chorus: Yah ribon olam v'olmayah, Ahnt hu malkah Melech malchayah.

Sh'vachin asadayr tzafrah v'ramshah,
Lach elahah kadishah, dee-v'rah kol nafshah,
Iyrin kadeeshin u'vnay enashah,
Chayvat b'rah v'ofay sh'mayah.

Chorus: Yah ribon olam...

Ravrvin ovdech v'takeefin
Mochich r'mayah v'zakif k'feefin,
Lu yichyeh g'var sh'nin alfin,
Loh yayol g'vurtaych b'chush-b'naiyah.

Chorus: Yah ribon olam...

Elahah dee lay, y'kar ur'vootah,
P'rok yat anach meepum ary'vatah,
V'apayk yat amaych meegoy galutah,
Amaych dee v'chart mikol umayah.

Chorus: Yah ribon olam...

L'mikda-shaych tuv ul'kodesh kudshin,
Asar dee vay yechedun ruchin v'nafshin,
Veezamrun loch sheerin v'racha-shin,
Beerush'laym kartah d'shufrayah.

Chorus: Yah ribon olam...

Master of the universe: You are the King, the King of kings; the work
of Your strength and the miracles, it is beautiful to declare before You. I
compose praise each morning and night, to You, O G-d, Who created all
life [including] the holy angels and humans, the animals of the field and
the birds of the heavens. Great and powerful are Your deeds, humbling
the haughty and straightening the bent. Even if humans would live
thousands of years, they would be unable to calculate Your greatness.
G-d to Whom is honor and greatness, redeem Your flock from the mouth
of the lions, take Your nation from exile, the nation that You have chosen
from all the others. Return to Your Sanctuary, to the Holy of Holies, the
place that souls and spirits will rejoice and sing to You songs and
praises—in Jerusalem, the city of beauty.

TZUR MEESHEH-LO
("The Rock from whose")

A 366 **B** 73 **BC** 297 **DP** 709

**Tzur meesheh-lo achalnu, barchu emunai,
Savanu v'hotarnu, kidvar Adonai.**

Chorus: **Tzur meesheh-lo achalnu, barchu emunai,
Savanu v'hotarnu, kidvar Adonai.**

**Hazan et olamo, Roaynu, Aveenu,
Achalnu et lachmo v'yayno shateenu,
Al kayn nodeh lishmo, un'hal'lo b'feenu,
Amarnu v'aneenu, ayn kadosh kaAdonai.**

Chorus: **Tzur meesheh-lo achalnu...**

**B'shir v'kol todah, n'varaych laylohaynu,
Al eretz chemdah tovah shehinchil laavotaynu,
Mazon v'tzaydah hisbiah l'nafshaynu,
Chasdo gavar alaynu, v'emet Adonai.**

Chorus: **Tzur meesheh-lo achalnu...**

**Rah-chaym b'chasdechah al amchah Tzuraynu,
Al tzeeyon mishkan k'vodecha, z'vul bayt tifartaynu,
Ben David avdecha yavo v'yigalaynu,
Ru-ach apaynu, m'shee-ach Adonai.**

Chorus: **Tzur meesheh-lo achalnu...**

Yeebaneh hamikdash, eer tzeeyon t'malay,

V'sham nashir shir chadash uvirnanah naaleh,
Harachaman hanikdash yitbaraych v'yitaleh,
Al kos yah-yin malay k'virkat Adonai.

Chorus: **Tzur meesheh-lo achalnu...**

The Rock whose food we have eaten, let us bless Him, my friends. We have eaten our fill and left over, according to G-d's word; He feeds the world, our Shepherd, our Father; we have eaten His bread and drunk His wine; therefore let us praise Him and sing loudly: "There is none as holy as G-d." Have mercy on Your nation in Your kindness; on Zion the resting place of Your glory, the shrine, home of our splendor; may the son of David, Your servant, come and redeem us; breath of our nostrils, messiah of G-d. Rebuild the temple, fill the city of Zion; there we will joyously sing a new song; let the Merciful, the Sanctified, be blessed over a cup brimming with wine, worthy of G-d's blessing.

HAVAYN YAKIR LEE

Havayn yakir lee Efra-yim,
im yeled sha-ashu-im,
kee meeday dabree bo zochor ezk'renu od.

Is it because Ephraim is my beloved son, or that he is such a lovely child, that—whenever I mention him—I yearn for him more and more?

HAMALACH HAGO-AYL

Hamalach hago-ayl otee mikol ra,
y'varaych et han'orim,
veey'koray vohem sh'mee
v'shaym avotai Avraham v'Yitzchak,
v'yidgu larov b'kerev ha-aretz.

May the angel who protects me from all evil bless the youngsters, and may their reputation become like mine and that of my fathers Abraham and Isaac, and may they teem in swarms in the land.

ACHAT SHO-ALTEE

Achat sho-altee may-ayt Hashem, otah avakaysh.
Shivtee b'vayt Hashem kol y'may cha-yai,
lachazot b'no-am Hashem ul'vakayr b'haychalo.

There is one thing that I ask of the Lord, one thing that I desire—that

I may dwell in the house of the Lord all the days of my life, witnessing the Lord's goodness and contemplating in His sanctuary.

ANEE MA-AMIN

Anee ma-amin b'emunah sh'laymah
b'veeyat hamashee-ach,
v'af al pee sheh-yitma-may-ah,
im kol zeh achakeh lo b'chol yom sheh-yavo.

I believe with perfect faith that the Messiah will come. And even if he may take his time, I will anticipate his arrival each and every day.

DOVID MELECH

Dovid melech Yisro-ayl chai v'kayam.

David, King of Israel, lives forever.

V'LEERUSHALAYIM IRCHA

V'leerushalayim ircha b'rachamim tashuv,
v'tishkon b'tochah ka-asher deebarta,
uv'nay otah b'korov b'yomaynu binyan olam,
v'cheesay Dovid m'hayrah l'tochah tachin.

Return, out of compassion, to Your city Jerusalem, and dwell in it as You said You would; rebuild it soon in our time as an everlasting structure, and swiftly establish David's throne.

L'MA-AN ACHAI

L'ma-an achai v'ray-ai, adabrah na shalom bach.
L'ma-an bayt Hashem Elokaynu avakshah tov lach.

For the sake of my brothers and friends, let me now talk of peace. For the sake of the house of the Lord our God, let me ask for good things for you.

L'SHANAH HABA-AH

L'shanah haba-ah beerushalayim hab'nu-yah.

Next year may we be in a rebuilt Jerusalem.

🪶 *Glossary* 🪶

Aliyah. Literally, "ascent." As used in the synagogue, *aliyah* refers to being called up to the Torah.

Amen. "It is true." Also an acronym for *El Melech Neeman*, "G-d is a faithful King." It is the response recited after a blessing, and indicates belief in the words of the blessing.

Amidah. "Standing." The silent prayer recited while standing, it is the most essential part of the prayer service. Also called *Shemoneh Esray.*

Amud. "Pillar." In the synagogue, it refers to the stand from which the *Chazan* (cantor) leads the congregation.

Aron Kodesh. "Holy closet." Always located at the front of the synagogue, it is the closet which houses the Torah scrolls.

Arvit. The evening prayer service. See *Maariv.*

Ba'al Koreh. "Master reader." A person trained in the intricacies of reading without cantillation and punctuation marks from the Torah scroll. This position was instituted so as not to embarrass those who are not proficient at reading from the Torah scroll when they are called up to the Torah.

Brachah. "Blessing." A *brachah* is a sanctification of G-d's Name, which can take the form of an expression of thanks, praise. One who hears a *brachah* recited is obligated to answer "*Amen.*"

Bimah. "Platform." The platform in the synagogue from which the Torah scroll is read.

Chazan (Ba'al Tefillah). "Cantor" ("master of prayer"). One who leads the congregation in prayer.

Emet. "Truth."

Hallel. "Praise."

Hashem. "The Name." A euphemistic way of referring to G-d.

Havdalah. "Separation." The ceremony performed at the conclusion of Shabbat which proclaims the division between Shabbat and the ensuing days of the week.

Kabbalat Shabbat. "Welcoming the Shabbat."

Kaddish. "Sanctification." An ancient prayer, mostly in Aramaic, which sanctifies G-d's Name. Recited by mourners as a benefit for the soul of the departed. The Talmud in many places discusses the cosmic effect of the congregation's response to *Kaddish*: *Y'hey Sh'may Rabbah M'varach L'alam Ul'almay Alamayah*, which declares our fervent wish that G-d's Name be sanctified forever.

Kiddush. Kiddush means "Sanctification," and one of the ways that we sanctify Shabbat is with wine. We say Kiddush in the Synagogue or at home before we eat.

Kohayn (singular), Kohanim (plural). "Priest." *Kohanim* is plural.) A descendant of Aaron, brother of Moses. The *Kohanim* were responsible for performing the sacrificial service in the Holy Temple. In our times, the *Kohanim* still act as G-d's servants by performing the Priestly Blessing over the congregation.

Kohayn Gadol. "High Priest." When the Holy Temple stood in Jerusalem, the *Kohayn Gadol* performed many of the most important Temple functions, such as the Yom Kippur service.

Levi. A descendant of the tribe of *Levi*, Jacob's third son. The Levites were appointed by G-d to serve as gatekeepers and musicians in the Holy Temple.

Maariv. In Hebrew this literally means "brings on [evening]" or "moves [the sun] to the West." The evening prayer service.

Maftir. "Conclusion." The person who receives the concluding *Aliyah* of the Torah reading, is called the *Maftir* since he is concluding the Torah reading. He does this by reading the section from the Prophets which corresponds with the portion read from the Torah in either meaning or subject matter.

Mechitzah. "Divider." The partition used in a synagogue in order to separate men and women.

Mezuzah. "Doorpost." A small scroll containing certain portions of the Torah, written according to exacting specifications, and affixed to the doorpost of every doorway leading into a living area.

Minchah. "Meal-offering." This is the afternoon prayer service, which replaced the afternoon offering in the Holy Temple.

Mitzvah (singular), Mitzvot (plural). "A commandment." The Torah describes 613 *mitzvot*, some requiring one to take a positive action, others requiring that we refrain from performing a certain action. It is the will of G-d that we follow every one of these commandments.

Mussaf. Literally, "additional" and refers to the additional prayer recited after the morning prayer on Shabbat and festivals. This prayer corresponds to the additional offering that was brought in the Holy Temple on these special days of the year.

Parsha (singular), Parshiyot (plural). "A division." A section of the Torah. Some *parshiyot* are "closed," meaning that a small space follows the end of the section in the Torah scroll, and the section begins on the same line. Other *parshiyot* are "open," meaning that the rest of the line in the Torah scroll is left open, and the following section begins on the next line.

Piyutim. Liturgical poems, most of these originate from the early centuries of the Common Era and from the Middle Ages. They were written for the special prayer services of the festival days. Their purpose is to highlight the themes of the day.

Sedrah. "[Part of a] series." The portion of the Torah read on Shabbat in the synagogue, sometimes referred to as *Parsha*.

Shacharit. "Morning." The morning prayer service.

Shemoneh Esray. See *Amidah*.

Simchat Torah. "The rejoicing over the Torah." The holiday immediately following *Succot* on which we celebrate the completion of the anuual Torah reading cycle.

Succah. Literally, "booth" or "tabernacle." A temporary residence built by Jews for the festival of *Succot*. A Jew is obligated to eat in the Succah for the duration of the seven-day holiday in order to recall the kindness of G-d in sheltering the Jews during their forty-year existence in the Wilderness. The succah also recognizes the fact that G-d provides us shelter from the vicissitudes of the harsh world around us.

Tallit (singular), Tallitot (plural). Literally, "garment." As used in the synagogue, it refers to the prayer shawl worn by men during the prayer service.

Talmud. Literally, "teaching." The oral explanation and discussion of the Mishnah, committed to writing and codified by Rav Ami and Rav Assi, heads of the Babylonian teaching academies, in the fifth century CE.

Tefillin. "Phylacteries." Small black leather boxes which contain certain Biblical passages, worn upon the arm and head of male Jews from the age of thirteen for weekday prayer services. While wearing *tefillin*, one is expected to maintain a clean body and absolutely pure thoughts.

Torah. Literally, "teaching." Strictly speaking, Torah refers only to the Five Books of Moses. However, all knowledge and teaching deriving from G-d's Revelation at Sinai is also collectively known as "Torah."

Tzitzit. "Fringes." The Torah commands that a male Jew attach fringes to a four-cornered garment, so that by seeing them, he will be reminded of G-d's commandments, in much the same way that a person ties a string around his finger to remind himself of something.

Yahrtzeit. "Yearly anniversary of a death."

Yisrael. As in *Kohayn, Levi, Yisrael.* This refers to the Children of Israel.